Design
and
Disability

Design and Disability

Edited by Natalie Kane
with Reuben Liebeskind

V&A Publishing

First published by V&A Publishing to accompany the exhibition *Design and Disability* on view from 7 June 2025 at the Victoria and Albert Museum, South Kensington, London SW7 2RL

This exhibition has been made possible as a result of the Government Indemnity Scheme. The V&A would like to thank HM Government for providing indemnity and the Department for Digital Culture, Media and Sport and Arts Council England for arranging the indemnity.

© Victoria and Albert Museum, 2025

Distributed in North America by Abrams, an imprint of ABRAMS
V&A publishing books are represented in UK and Europe by Abrams & Chronicle Books, 1 West Smithfield, London, EC1A 9JU and 57 rue Gaston Tessier, 75166 Paris, France.
 www.abramsandchronicle.co.uk
 info@abramsandchronicle.co.uk

ISBN 978 1 83851 0572

10 9 8 7 6 5 4 3 2 1
2029 2028 2027 2026 2025

A catalogue record for this book is available from the British Library.

Every effort has been made to seek permission to reproduce those images whose copyright does not reside with the V&A, and we are grateful to the individuals and institutions who have assisted in this task. Any omissions are entirely unintentional, and the details should be addressed to V&A Publishing.

Designer: Joe Ewart
Copy editor: Jessica Spencer
Printed in Italy by Printer Trento
Reprographics by Dexter Premedia

V&\ Publishing
The power of creativity
Discover more at vam.ac.uk

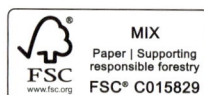

FSC
www.fsc.org

MIX
Paper | Supporting responsible forestry
FSC® C015829

Foreword

In every era, design has served as a reflection of society's values, aspirations, and power structures. From its founding in 1852, the V&A has championed creative design and sought to democratize public access to collections and knowledge.

Design and Disability invites us to re-examine popular design narratives by centring the experiences and expertise of Disabled, Deaf, and Neurodivergent people. The exhibition challenges the narrative that disability is an 'issue' to be 'solved' or 'overcome' through design. Instead, it celebrates disability as a vibrant culture and identity – one that enriches and informs design innovation.

This publication compels us to recognize that design is not a neutral practice. Every line drawn, every structure built, and every tool created reflects the dynamics of societal power. In turning our attention to disability-first design practices, we uncover a history where creativity is deeply intertwined with the everyday experiences of those who navigate the world in ways that diverge from and challenge dominant structures. By foregrounding these perspectives, *Design and Disability* not only charts a course for a more equitable design future but also redefines what it means to innovate.

The narrative presented here is brought together through interviews, essays and project spotlights to reveal the myriad ways in which disabled people have actively shaped design. From the insightful developments of urban neighbourhoods to the transformative role of graphic design and typography as tools of activism, this book underscores a profound truth: disabled people have always been, and continue to be, essential contributors to design and cultural production. Their expertise is a powerful demonstration of designing from lived experience.

At its core, this publication is about visibility and agency – underscored by the use of the Zed typeface and cream-tinted paper, ensuring that the knowledge shared within these pages is truly available to all. It highlights how design and its accompanying practices can be reimagined when we question established norms. By presenting design challenges and provocations from a disability-first perspective, we learn to see the built environment not merely as a backdrop for life, but as an active participant in shaping our daily experiences. The examples showcased here offer creative alternatives that benefit the entire field of design, expanding our understanding of what is possible when inclusivity is woven into every stage of creation.

In this spirit, *Design and Disability* serves as a rich resource for designers, architects, educators and policymakers who are eager to explore inclusive design practices. It paves the way for a more inclusive society by emphasizing that the design process itself must be as diverse as the communities it serves.

We are very grateful to everyone at Oak Foundation for their generosity towards this exhibition.

Tristram Hunt
Director, V&A

Introduction

Design is, in essence, about solutions and creativity. In fact it's fair to say that the history of design is littered with failures. For disabled people design in its broadest sense can mean that the made world is often one to reckon with and negotiate, rather than participate in. Throughout history, dominant systems of design have excluded us from the beginning of the design process, resulting in a world that doesn't acknowledge or enable us and which refuses to offer autonomy and justice. By ignoring disabled experience, the designed world has become a series of barriers – be it inaccessible buildings, information culture or clothing. This world can mean both a lack of access to public life and a lack of independence in private.[1]

This book aims to contribute to the conversation on the future of design and disabled cultural production by building knowledge through the stories it tells. It aims to demonstrate how disability can and must be embedded in every stage of design and production by drawing on the expertise of users themselves. Across the interviews, projects and essays that follow, what design is, can and even should be is presented through disabled, Deaf and neurodivergent lenses. Each chapter goes further in expanding design histories and contemporary design narratives, firmly acknowledging disabled design practices as part of the story, and showing the richness of disabled expertise in its many forms. This expertise has been erased from design wherever disabled experience has been deprioritized or devalued. The book draws on the embodied knowledge and lived experiences of its disabled, Deaf and neurodivergent contributors, and their understanding of the vital work of access and community building.

The practitioners throughout these chapters are engaged in acts of manoeuvring around, even breaking, an ecosystem of design that restricts, negates or excludes disabled experience or use. Design, in many ways, is about world-building because the purpose of engaging with design methods is to make objects, systems and realities that do not currently exist. For disabled people, it is an act of 'misfitting' – challenging an environment that is at odds with one's own lived experience – that often spurs this reimagining of our material things.[2] What worlds do we want to inhabit. What futures do we want to imagine and exist within?

The answers to these questions often come from people who are not typically considered designers or makers themselves, but who are equally vital to the work of activating design cultures. In **How to Build a Network**, the Instagram account Adaptive Hacks – organized, maintained and, in many ways, celebrated by Mary Slattery – explores the everyday design contributions of disabled people. Slattery pushes against 'technoableism' by sharing objects and tools that have been repurposed, retooled and augmented to make them usable by members of her Instagram community.[3] Design teams all too often relegate disabled people to being consultants and focus-group participants, rather than makers or authors in their own right.[4] What we often see is a designed world full with objects, or 'Disability Dongles' that look helpful or well-meaning but aren't.[5]

In **How to Play a Game** writer Grant Stoner examines a particular community of designer–users – videogame players – highlighting the multiple points at which access is denied and users are failed, especially by industrial-scale design. He writes about how communities of players have customized and created adaptive set-ups and controllers, sometimes succeeding in forcing change on industry. There is always a tension between those who design games and the disabled user, particularly those who are already playing the game of their own access needs, literally and metaphorically, and many of whom are at the mercy of the latest trend or controller lifecycle. Who wins will always be a question of whose priorities are valued – disabled players or shareholders.

In **How to Design a Font** two designers subvert graphic design to probe the intersection of access, aesthetics and representation. Emily Sara, in pulling shapes out of activist archives to create something new in her 504 font, enables a further dialogue to occur, extending history in two directions – both remembrance and possibility. In building the pieces of the 504 font from many disjointed parts of posters and placards, Emily Sara references disability studies scholar Tobin Siebers's concept of 'disability aesthetics', which, in his words, 'embraces beauty that seems by traditional standards to be broken, and yet it is not less beautiful, but more so, as a result.'[6] In pushing back against graphic standards of harmony or even legibility, the 504 font gives access to history and community.

Conor Foran's Dysfluent Mono is a typography that is perhaps only truly activated when used to represent an individual's speech. Designed to represent the spoken word of a person with a stammer, it interrogates our assumptions about reading and gives life to a page – particularly when with communication disabilities there is a tendency to edit, reduce, smooth as words are recorded to a page. As a result each interview in *Dysfluent*, Foran's magazine, becomes an intimate, singular portrait through type – a unique exercise when type is so often given to universality.

Both the 504 font and Dysfluent Mono become a form of what could be called crip archiving – whereby the design of each type itself becomes a means to archive disabled cultural experience. Both demonstrate where graphic design and type have been vital records across countless engagements with political life, whether on posters in protest movements or pushing back against ableist technology.

How to Design a Neighbourhood and **How to Build a House** respectively explore ways of being together in places of shared living and ways of building in light of the contributions of disabled experience. For the team behind the neighbourhood Block Party: From Independent Living to Disability Communalism, the importance of acknowledging and folding disabled community knowledge, past, present and future, into plans for a space is vital. This project acknowledged the importance of balancing and meeting multiple perspectives and needs. This perhaps indicates a movement towards what Elizabeth Guffey calls 'post-Universal Design', which rejects some of its predecessor's limited approaches and histories to embrace something altogether more complex, intersectional and critical.[7]

Jordan Whitewood-Neal and Christopher Laing discuss in their chapter, **How to Build a House**, how nothing sits in isolation when considering the role of architecture in our lives. Though there is no single disabled 'community' – no monolithic culture – community is an important aspect when it comes to imagining broader, better possibilities, particularly when considering how intersectional and antiracist living can be enacted. Irene Cheng, one of Block Party's designers, emphasizes the role of 'communal flourishing' in the design of Block Party's neighbourhood, whereby meeting multiple access needs can enable creativity, joy and better political and social lives.

This idea is continued in **How to Start a Club** – a conversation between Finnegan Shannon and Poppy Levison in which both highlight the importance of what Levison refers to as 'cross-disability solidarity' in design, which acknowledges what multiple disabled-led perspectives, and their negotiation,

bring to critiques of space.[8] In the case of Finnegan's project, the Anti-Stairs Club Lounge, this started with a protest against a structure – Thomas Heatherwick's Vessel – that inherently rejects disabled participation because stairs are fundamental to how the building is used. There was no quick solution to the problems of that building, but the protest resulted in the formation of a club or movement – something larger to enable a wider critique of urban design and the political landscape it reflects.

Disabled people have always sought, and found, solutions to the realities of their lives, often by communal action and regardless of the political or economic landscape. A response to a rapidly changing landscape of disabled-led activism is explored in **How to Protest**. The DIY Proxy Protest Power Tool responds to the need for greater access to political life for disabled people, and was developed with agile, safe community use in mind – its appropriation of encrypted and easily available mobile-phone-based tools enable disabled people to participate in protest though a proxy. It emphasizes how access technologies are critical, especially when it comes to examining the power dynamics at play as disabled communities intersect with political systems.

Testing, pushing and breaking design have become necessary tools in fighting design injustice for disabled communities. Transport networks have been disrupted by disabled passengers across the world by those who couldn't use them, from the Kawasaki prefecture protests in Japan in 1977,[9] to action in South Korea since 2001.[10] In 2023 Rishi Sunak's Conservative government in the UK implemented protest laws that included the criminalization of action that involves 'locking on' with items such as handcuffs or disrupting 'major transport works'. Such a law in the 1990s would have made many of the groundbreaking protests by organizations in the UK such as Disabled People's Direct Action Network (DAN) significantly more difficult and risky for those taking part, potentially slowing down the changes made to transport infrastructure as a result of their actions. The DIY Proxy Protest Power Tool shows how the subversion of existing design continues to be a necessary mechanism in achieving political momentum towards the designed world that disabled people want.

Further venturing into digital spaces, in **How to Make an Image** Jameisha Prescod and Reuben Liebeskind talk about subverting and converting hyper-consumerist online platforms – in this case Instagram – into spaces for community care and advocacy. For Prescod this means ensuring that those who are often most marginalized, particularly Black disabled communities, claim agency over the way they are portrayed, particularly where algorithmic processes may work against them. While also serving to share important community health knowledge, Prescod's platform promotes and celebrates disabled visibility as a means of collective liberation.

In **How to Dress Well** the complexity of visibility – what we choose to reveal, or not, through the choices we make – is navigated through dress by fashion scholar Ben Barry. Countless disabled fashion cultures have emerged over time embracing the items we wear as a creative possibility rather than a solution to the 'problem' of disability. Centring disabled-led practices and creativity adds a new dimension to an industry that already has a complicated relationship to body politics. A disability-first, intersectional engagement with dress would enable a full spectrum of choice, reflecting and holding all disabled life and desire.

In a group discussion between directors and members of artist studio Intoart in **How to Start a Studio**, member Nancy Clayton talks about how art is power and how mainstream arts education fails disabled people and fails to use their expertise. Intoart, consisting of a cohort of learning disabled and autistic artists, designers and makers, uses multiple access points as the support frame for exploration, before building vital community and peer networks around a rigorous pedagogy. Intoart's Trifle Studio provides an important way for learning disabled practitioners to join the industry, on their own terms, through multidisciplinary design collaborations. Like many other artist groups in history such as the Bloomsbury Group and the Bauhaus, Intoart has established its own movement with a style and aesthetic born out of the artists' connections to each other, their research and material interests.

Art activist and disabled campaigner Jen White-Johnson's *Anti Ableist Art Educators Manifesto* (2022) states that 'Art is our survival'. To be part of deep creative ecologies – whether in art schools or design studios or as part of a wider community encouraging adaptation/improvements to existing designs – is vital to ensuring that disabled communities continue to be represented in history and in society.[11]

This book aims to be part of this creative ecology. The chapters, though didactic in their titles, should be considered a series of open possibilities. To take any as a fixed solution to a fixed problem would be to miss the point. Collectively the authors and their communities invite you to consider a disability critique of design and, in doing so, to go to where design has previously marginalized disabled perspectives. Established structures of design are enmeshed with capitalism, the goals of productivity, individualism, extractivism and hyper-consumerism, all of which are inherently antithetical to disabled, Deaf and neurodivergent lives.[12] While these factors have rendered us an error in the system, the pages of this book instead detail disability as a site of creative possibility. We all need to imagine otherwise. In this book, terminology varies according to how a person may define themselves and/or their community as it has been important for preferences to be prioritized. Speech patterns have also

been honoured as much as possible. At the back of this book is a glossary, where you'll find useful terms, and a reading list to continue your learning.

How to Build a Network

Interview between Arjun Harrison-Mann and Mary Slattery

How do you invent the world you want to live in, with others? In this conversation, Arjun and Mary explore the creativity of disabled-led networks that reimagine, subvert and repurpose existing designs. Through using social media platforms such as Instagram in ways not originally intended, Slattery's platform Adaptive Hacks encourages disabled people to come together to reflect on their own experiences with design and unite in finding disabled joy.

Arjun: I've been following Adaptive Hacks for a while and it's impressive to see your approach and the level of care you take in supporting people through this network. In particular how the systems you facilitate relate to a wide range of lived experiences and access requirements, as well as the hopes and dreams that are reflected through each design object. I was wondering if you could tell us a bit about the origins, or the ethos that went into forming Adaptive Hacks?

Mary: I set up its sister page Adaptive Meals on a whim one day because I just recognized a need. I often go through long periods where I really can't work out what food is safe for my body to eat, because sometimes it seems to hate all food, and I was talking to friends about the different barriers around eating and drinking, and the best way for me to do anything is impulsively. So I set up the disabled meals page. It grew to, I think, 3000 followers in a day and I was really overwhelmed, but then I recognized that, by just talking about meals, it sort of meant that lots of conversations were half finished and lots of people's barriers weren't just food or drink. And so I set up the other page, which originally was called Disabled Hacks.

Even though we are disabled people, and I don't think it's wrong to use 'disabled' as a broad term, I also want to be as intentional as possible about language at all times. I used Adaptive Hacks and Adaptive Meals as a way to reflect where I want to sit with my

language politics – about how we're inventors and pirates and punks. I just find that a really exciting way to think about us and a way to empower us, away from the old models of thinking about disability – the charity model and the medical model and things. I think 'adaptive' is a really nice way to remove us from those histories and their contemporary realities.

Arjun: This speaks really well to the importance of designing from people's own experience, and how the act of designing, creating or adapting can, at times, become a cathartic experience. Is this something that you feel resonates with the making of these pages?

Mary: I often operate quite close to my capacity due to how unwell I am and how unmet my needs are by the state. So I find just setting up a social media account means that I don't have to know any web design or pay for anything or spend ages doing any preparation. It's quick and dirty. It can go from an idea to a tool that exists in five minutes maximum. Because of my other accounts, I can immediately tell quite a lot of people about it, whereas, for me, having to do something that requires learning a new skill or arranging a time to work with someone else who has a skill that I don't have – I just don't have capacity in my life to be involved in things that have multi-step planning and organizing and learning. And I certainly don't have the material resources to buy a web-hosting site or Squarespace account.

Arjun: You started a page on Adaptive Meals and then expanded it to address the further barriers that sat on the periphery of food and drink. Often designers think that the process of design ends at the production of a tool or product, but the way that tool is interacted with, whether intentionally or not, is as much an important design opportunity as its physicality is. This is something I believe your page achieves through the way it highlights, challenges and addresses existing designed barriers.

Mary: I don't tend to think about it from that perspective. I have a social-care package, and I have an occupational therapist, and stuff, from the council so I think in terms that relate to disability – and my politics about disability has been formed as a reaction to my lived experience.

The DWP (Department for Work and Pensions) or social services or the NHS will say the only thing that's important is that you manage to get your socks on. It doesn't matter whether you feel good or OK or like you've got any self esteem. It just doesn't matter if you're OK or not. It matters that the socks are on, but for me it really matters that someone is OK and that they feel good, because disability is so underserved and ignored and we live in such a society where it's really easy to dismiss disabled people.

I really notice, when I interact with other disabled people, particularly strangers, that the skills and knowledge that we've developed around our experiences are low value, a bit embarrassing, should be kept secret. And one of the things that is really exciting about the project is that I get to respond to someone saying, 'Oh, I don't know if this is helpful, but this is the way that I do it,' by saying, 'Wow, that is incredibly innovative. How brilliant. You're amazing. How did you come up with that? How did you learn how to melt that tool and reshape it safely in your own home? That's incredible.' There's a perception of disabled people as lacking grit, determination, imagination, strength of character. My page completely exposes what a load of shit that is, because all the people interacting with the page display the inaccuracy of those criticisms. They show all their strengths, innovativeness, generosity, cleverness in bounds and I get to name it.

Something that I notice a lot is that, because I don't have a career and a job, I don't have a place where people tell me I'm good at anything, ever. I go to the hospital where people are cross with me or the doctor's surgery where people are cross with me or I interact with the DWP where people are cross with me. Or I interact with people I really love who are hurt that I'm too poorly to do the thing they want, or I interact with neighbours who are really angry that I have a disabled-parking bay and they don't have their own bay. There's something really important about giving disabled people a space where everyone isn't cross with them and telling them that they're wrong and they shouldn't be here.

adaptivemeals ...

When i feel sick or sensory overload.
I have just pasta, oil and salt.
Surprisingly tasty and a very safe
food for me.

▶ Photo

adaptivemeals ...

I always turn to ice lollies/pops when
nausea or sickness is really bad and
the thought of solids is too much, or I
can't keep anything down. As they hit
your system slower I find I at least
keep some sugar and hydration in me
💛 my mum found this when I was
first poorly as a child. Bonus points
for lime flavour Callipos!

adaptivemeals ...

Select a location to see product availability
ZXBAERS zxbaers Electric Mini Garlic Chopper,
250ML Portable USB Waterproof...
$14.99 prime Sponsored
Visit the Chef'n Store ★★★★☆ 4,285
Chef'n VeggiChop Hand-Powered Food Chopper (Arugula)
Amazon's Choice in Seasoning & Spice Choppers by C...

2 Colors:
Arugula

1. I'm so glad this exists ❤️❤️❤️
2. This is a pull chopper, it's saved so
much time and mental energy when
chopping and is easier than pushing
down. I used to just each chunks of
garlic and ginger but now it's so easy
to properly dice stuff 😌

adaptivemeals ...

I also use a Tefal soup maker. It's so
easy, you literally just put vegetables
and stock in it, and it cooks it for you.
You can choose chunky or smooth
soup options.

TEFAL EASY SOUP BL841140 SOUP
MAKER / STAINLESS STEEL & WHITE
REFERENCE : BL841140

19

I identify as mad and I've been harmed by the mental-health system through neglect. The opportunity to empower people, and sneak in some radical mental-health care through making people who are made to feel worthless and like they shouldn't be alive feel valuable and important and exciting, is really healing for me.

Arjun: This notion of radical care feels so present on your page, and another key thing that comes through is the joy or excitement when a tool or hack breaks down a barrier. Such as microfibre gloves for accessible dusting, or collapsible stools for resting in public spaces.

Mary: A lot of disabled people that I meet really resonate with the phrase 'disabled joy' – it means a lot to us. It's a very specific type of joy that is different to the joy we were taught about in films and books and fairy tales. It's really special and singular, and it's so nice for me when my work can bring little bits of joy.

Arjun: Can we reflect on Adaptive Hacks as a network disseminating open-source knowledge, particularly grassroot hacks, methods for subverting design objects and building a culture via networks that highlight the necessity for anti-ableist design? I wonder if you could say a bit about where you see Adaptive Hacks sitting between being a tool, a service or a provocation?

Mary: I'm sorry that this is a boring answer, but I really feel like it's all three. I want, at its core, for it to be a tool, and then other things to be byproducts. One of the things I find really hard about the model is that it puts me in this role that I don't really want to be in. I would really like it to be self-sustaining and I would love it to exist on a different platform where there doesn't need to be a me. Or maybe there's a group of facilitators who just check that things are safe, but otherwise it's that people can post their own things and other people can respond – like Reddit, I guess.

But yeah, it's rooted in radical politics. The word that I know I use a lot is 'prefigurative', because that's really what it is. For me it's creating something that I needed to exist in the world and then seeing how other people, with different needs, need it to exist in the world. And sort of gradually trying to shape it – to meet different needs that I didn't previously understand or encounter in my own life.

I do find Instagram a really difficult place because if I think about those three words that you used – it could be more than those things if it existed in a different space. But because it's on Instagram it has a sort of petty dictatorship feeling to it, because I control what's posted, when it's posted, who posts, what language they use, what everything looks like, and I don't want to. I don't crave power in any way over anyone, except my own experience. I find it really hard that the only tool that's accessible and affordable to me is Instagram and the model of it is that every single person with an account runs

adaptivemeals

Hi! This is the Spill-Not (you can get from Amazon) it is LITERALLY the best invention ever for people with mobility instability and balance issues. It uses centrifugal force to keep your mug from spilling.

adaptivemeals

Vegetable cutting cradle

EAKING NEWS   BREA

I cut a potato!

adaptivehacks

Telescopic collapsible stool - available in many colours.

I have found a life changing product, on Amazon for ~£20.
Search 'Telescopic Collapsable Stool'. It folds to the size of a small bag, is very light, and has a strap to carry over your shoulder. It can be opened up to the height of a normal seat and used mid walk or in queues to rest. The type I have holds up to 130kg but there is some variation across brands by -20kg

adaptivemeals and adaptivehacks

Eazyhold tool grippers

eazyhold

their own tiny dictatorship, and I don't want to do that.

Arjun: These are the important challenges that come with using platforms that are rooted in capitalism or rooted in this kind of exchange, right? I think that's why the term 'subversion' is so important, because it's the idea of taking something and reusing it in a way that it wasn't originally intended. Which I think brings us to this idea of prefigurative design that you mention – enacting the reality you want to see happen now. You said you wouldn't describe it as a tool, a service and a provocation. What language would you use to describe Adaptive Hacks?

Mary: How would I describe it in my own words? I have a real bias towards trying to use the plainest English possible – partly because of not being able to go to college and university and stuff, and partly because I want everything to be super accessible all the time and really translatable to other languages. So I would probably say it's a social media page where anyone can send in a message asking any question, and a really important rule is that there is nothing that's embarrassing or wrong or gross – I want people to ask me about the most taboo aspects of disability. I really, really love working with the more taboo subjects: I want to do all the toilet stuff, I want to do all the personal hygiene stuff, the sex disasters or whatever. So, yeah, it's like, problem-solving and taboo-breaking whilst modelling an unapologetic,

shame-free way to exist with access needs.

Arjun: I think that leads us very well into the next conversation, which is more about this idea of networks and community.

Mary: I often really feel uncomfortable with how 'community' is used in, sort of, social justice conversations. People will say 'the disabled community' or the 'insert-any-identity community' and then I think about the people I know and how they would, technically, be considered a part of that community because they share that identity label, but then wouldn't necessarily feel included because of, maybe, multiple marginalizations. And so, actually, 'network' is such a nice word to use instead, where community feels like … You know … I do actually live in a very strong community. I've lived in this neighbourhood for 20 years and I know all my neighbours and I know everything that goes on in the neighbourhood, and we all look after each other. I have a disabled neighbour who lives opposite me – and she phones me if my curtains are still closed by lunchtime. She's like, 'Mary? Are you OK? What's happening?' And so, when I think about what community means, I think about that. It's really tangible. It's really keeping me alive. I'm keeping them alive. My neighbours – we all share everything and we're really around for the long haul in each other's lives, through messy things and across religious and cultural and political barriers.

adaptivehacks

hanging dry laundry if the storage is out of reach?

Anyone have household object or hack for getting clothes hung up on high rack? I remember retails stores having poles with hooks

adaptivehacks

Accessible crochet?

Hi Mary! Looking for hacks/magical tips for crochet- specifically the non-dominant hand holding the project as you work. Not tension, not hooks, and not the movement. The pincer grip between thumb and index as it grips the piece you're working on. I have muscle death in both hands from being too nerdy of a teen, so I can't touch my thumbs to fingertips- essentially what the grip is. Thanks!

adaptivehacks

Use makeup sponges to create ergonomic handles!

Cheap way to make an ergonomic rochet hook using make up sponges.

For the person who spoke about struggling to hold their projects because of the pincer grip..... get a pair of the glasses holders that your wear around your neck, put some little plastic stitch holders in the end and you can attach it to your crochet project and hang it around your neck so it stays still. (Sadly I don't have a photo of that)

♡ ○ ▽   🔖

Liked by **nina_tame** and **151 others**
adaptivehacks Hack from @clairey_cluck

adaptivehacks

Salah Chair

Mobility aid for praying Muslim people.

Sometimes I find it really hard, and maybe it's just the autism, when people use 'community' very broadly, about a group of people who have nothing in common except how they look, or something. Does that make a community? I don't think so. And I think it's dangerous when we use a word with such an important meaning in loads of different ways, including ways that feel a bit meaningless to me.

Arjun: A core phrase we hear across disability justice movements is 'Nothing About Us Without Us', which speaks to the need for disabled people to be an integral part of design processes and networks. What would you like this role to be, or your role to be within this network?

Mary: I'm not sure. I guess I would love everything to be by consensus, because that's more aligned with my politics, but I don't have capacity to facilitate everything that happens on the page. One of the ways that I'm looking to address that at the moment is that I'm going to set up an agreement – hopefully with a small group of people – that they participate more, in exchange for me giving them references for jobs or education, because it's really difficult for a lot of disabled people to get any work experience and references. I'm really hoping that I can help people to get that and help build their self-esteem and apply for things if I give them more of a role in these projects. One of the ways that it could be really accessible for me is if it's not formalized in any way. I just say, 'Please turn on your notifications

for these pages and, whenever there's a post, please help it reach people and contribute as much as you can to helping this person solve their problem.'

'Disability rights' – which I don't use – is a liberal concept, based on the idea that, if people have rights, liberation and equality will naturally emerge, and I don't believe that at all. I think that rights hold us back in many ways, because they give the illusion of liberation and justice whilst enabling the injustice to carry on at pace, doing its thing. I use 'disability justice' because I really want justice and liberation. I was thinking that prisons are filled with disabled people who are criminalized for existing in unruly bodies and minds and incarcerated. Disabled people have rights, but no justice, and really limited liberation. And so I would say nothing that I do is rooted in disability rights. Everything is rooted in disability justice as much as possible. I'm sure I get it wrong because I have never existed in any context other than a liberal society, and so I don't know how to be 'maximum abolitionist', but I'm trying my best.

One of the things that I think about loads in the design of the page and how it works is that Instagram is based in America. The majority of the users on English-language Instagram are in America. So a lot of the work is about trying to manage how much space American needs and products take up, because I'm really aware of American cultural imperialism and the impact it has. I try to get more ideas, more solutions, more stories about what disability means for people in all sorts of different cultures.

The more that I can decentre the so-called West and focus on global minority populations, the more excited I get about the project. I also do work with rich white people, who are the people who take up the most space and ask the most questions and require the most labour, to try to help them understand how important it is that I decentre them in projects. I also try to really think about the companies and products that we're promoting and how we talk about different companies. I'm really careful to ask people not to make a big performance of saying how terrible it is to shop from Amazon, but then also really support people talking about boycott movements when they're talking about where to get products.

Arjun: The stuff you're doing works on so many different levels. Adaptive Hacks is an ecology of tools and hacks, but also a project that subverts Instagram's capitalistic purpose as a social media platform in order to purposefully foreground a wide range of disabled people's experiences. Reflecting on some of these objects, I was wondering if there was an Adaptive Hacks design manifesto. What do you reckon some of its key points might be?

Mary: Expertise comes from lived experience before anything else. Decentring professionals like healthcare professionals and occupational therapists – I want to hear disabled voices first and I don't really want to hear from anyone with any traditional claims to power and expertise without lived experience. The aesthetic of the page will always be deprioritized, below accessibility, and that means not just accessibility for the reader but for me as a very energy-limited person. No pity, no apologies, no deference, no shame, no charity. We're all equal. We're all powerful. Being as kind and humane to each other as possible. Acknowledging power imbalances in order to create safety and equality – I don't think you can just assume that we're all going to treat each other OK, because we're not. We have had to keep saying racism exists, therefore I'm doing *this* all the time. I really, really believe: name it, name it, name it all the time.

And one of the things I'm extremely motivated by in all of my work is that I had to figure it all out alone, for decades and decades, in poverty, before I found all this community exploding in 2018. And so it's a lot about what I wish someone had taken me aside and told me – about what it means to be disabled and what really basic tools I need and what basic language I need. Yeah, just trying to create the world that I need to live in every day, through every choice on that page.

Is that the kind of thing you'd put in a design manifesto?

Arjun: Oh, I think it needs to be.

How to Play a Game

2

Essay by Grant Stoner

Many of us play videogames, whether it's to blow off steam at the end of the day or as serious competitive gamers, but access isn't equitable for everyone. Games journalist Grant Stoner takes us through his life using games controllers, from hacking devices as a teenager with his brother to experimenting with the latest industry innovations. He examines the ways in which disabled communities far outpace games companies in creativity and ambition.

Facing page:
Accessible packaging for the Xbox Adaptive Controller.

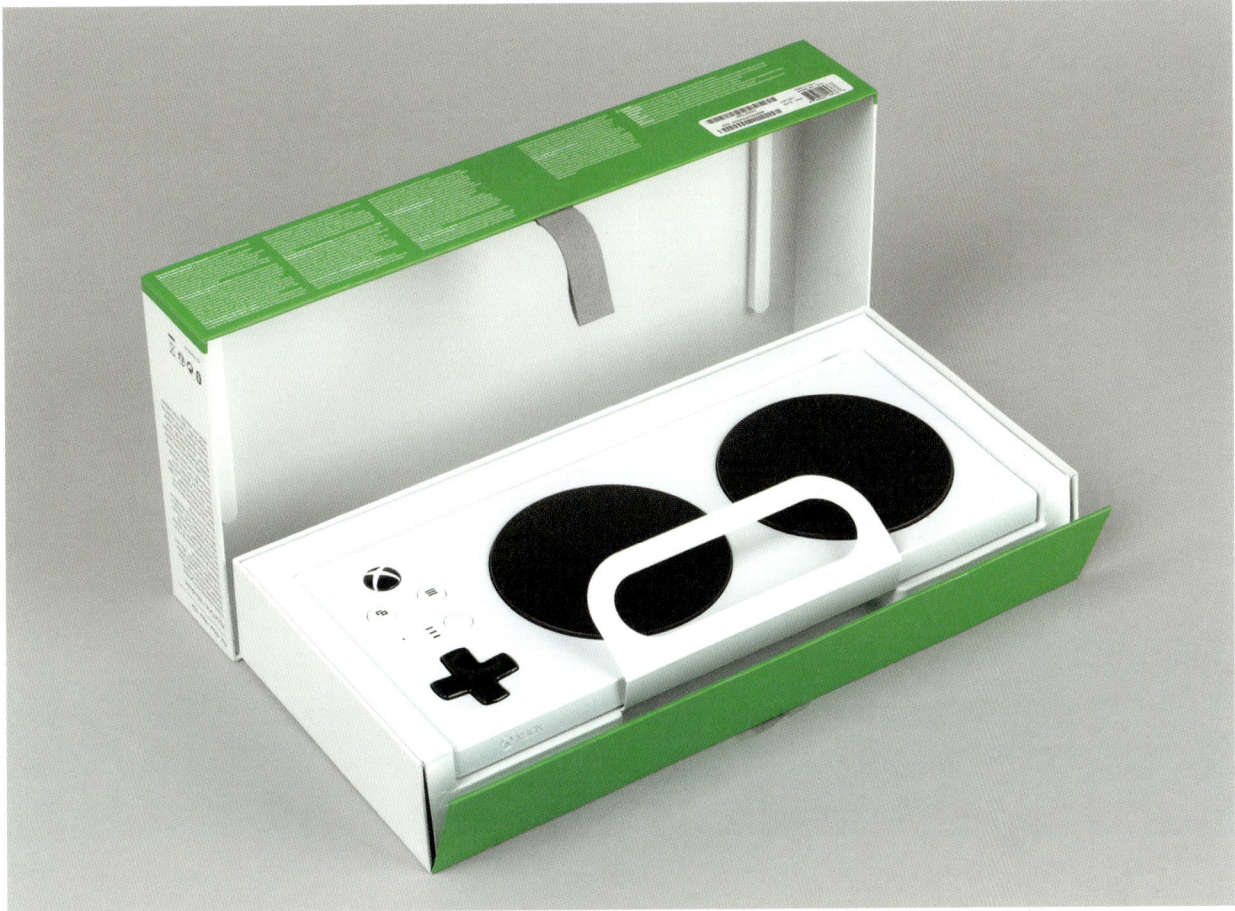

The disabled experience is incredibly individual and constantly evolving. Even people with the same disability will interact in vastly different ways with the same medium, and that includes games and games consoles. Accessibility requires far more than dozens of options hidden away in different menus. While software is important – and new design innovations are finally allowing more disabled individuals to play games – hardware is crucial to accessibility and the industry response remains disappointing.

Each individual plays games with the settings that best suit their specific needs, including customizable subtitles, button remapping and even audio cues for objects and enemies. This is especially true with hardware like videogame controllers. These are as important as the systems they operate. Each player has their favourite. From the Gamecube Wavebird in 2003 to the first iteration of the Xbox 360 controller in 2007, the pads we play on help to define each console generation. The controller, with its ergonomic design, button layout

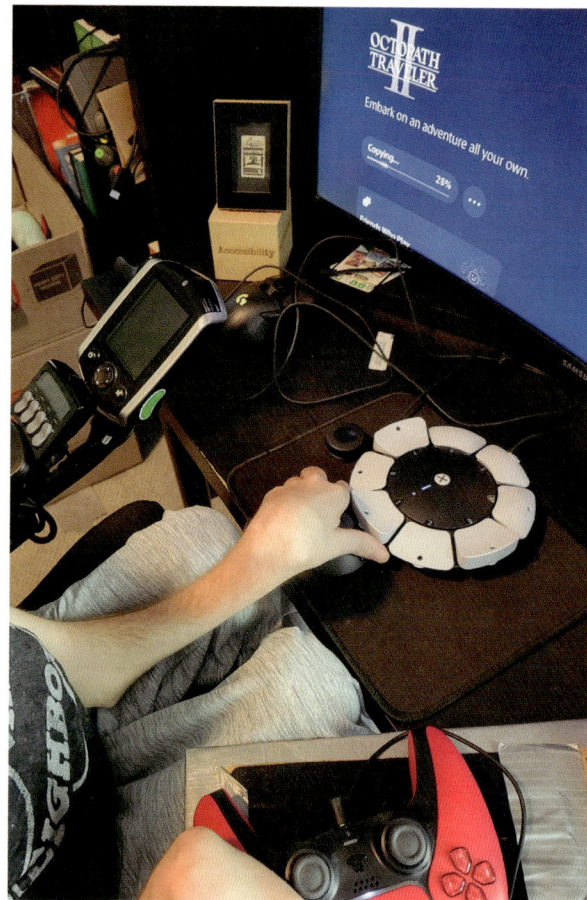

and control-stick positioning, is always the entry point to playing any game. Yet, for disabled individuals, gaming hardware can be both a blessing and an inaccessible nightmare.

While software and designs are exclusive to specific game companies, hardware can be acquired through companies like Xbox or PlayStation, or even through third-party creators and organizations like SpecialEffect. Standard controllers

Above left: Xbox Adaptive Controller with Logitech Adaptive Gaming Kit switches and buttons.
Above right: PlayStation Access Controller.

are no longer the norm. For physically disabled players especially, an inaccessible piece of hardware can completely ruin the experience. Even with a bevy of accessible options and inclusive design practices in most modern games software, the hardware is crucial. During my journey with gaming controllers, there have been improvements in first-party equipment, by which I mean equipment made by the main brand manufacturers. They have responded to requests for better hardware, and devices are rapidly becoming more accessible – and yet they still feature numerous flaws.

Evolving Equipment

As someone with a progressive disease – spinal muscular atrophy type II – I'm all too familiar with needing specialized equipment and outside assistance. I cannot perform simple tasks like feeding, dressing or bathing without help, and these limitations certainly impact other areas of my life, including gaming. Growing up, I could utilize most controllers with ease. While I occasionally struggled with pressing certain buttons, like R1, R2, L1 and L2 – crucial for functions like aiming and firing weapons – on my DualShock 2 device, my strength and range of motion had yet to properly impact my hands. However, even as the gaming industry and its technology progressed, so did my disability.

I was first made aware of my physical gaming needs when my brother and I purchased the Xbox 360 in 2007. While the sticks and face buttons were perfect for me, arguably better than any controller used previously, I was unable to reach the right trigger because of my atrophied hands. And, at a time when the industry had yet to implement standard accessibility settings, if a game relied extensively on that specific trigger, I was forced to either ask for outside assistance or abandon the game altogether. My brother, an avid gamer

Top right: Xbox 360 controller with popsicle adaptation.
Bottom right: Playstation's DualShock 4 controller by Evil Genius.

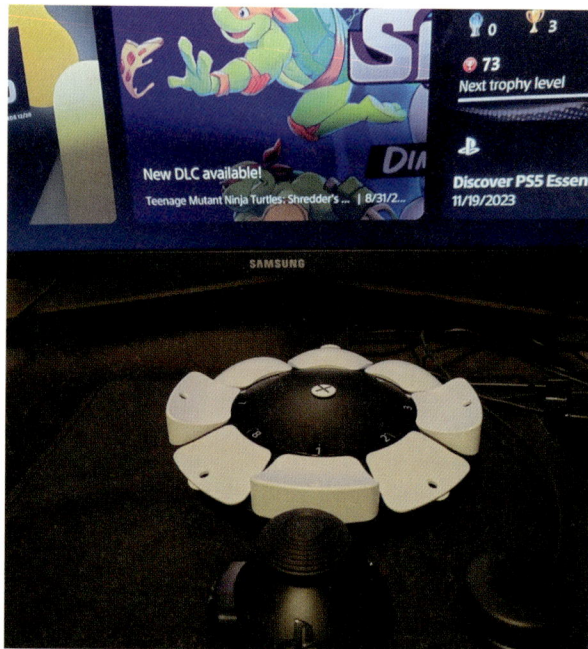

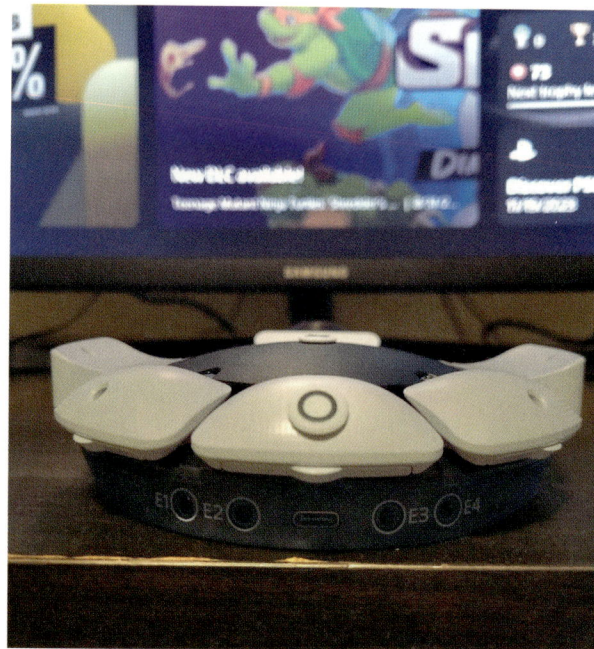

himself, used electrical tape and a simple popsicle stick taped to the back of the controller allowing me to use the homemade device as a makeshift lever. For years, this worked with no issues, aside from needing to occasionally apply more tape. But this was only possible because of the Xbox 360 controller's overall design and the strength in my hands. When the console market eventually shifted to a new generation, with heavier controllers, tougher buttons and less ergonomic shapes, new issues arose.

A progressive disability means that my strength or range of motion can worsen at any moment. When the

PlayStation 4 console was released in 2013, its design meant I no longer had the capability to press the bumpers or triggers. Coinciding with this was the new design of the DualShock 4 (the controller for the PlayStation), which prevented my brother from using the same popsicle stick method that I had grown accustomed to for approximately seven years. For the first time in my life, I looked for outside assistance beyond my family and friends. Thankfully, a company known as Evil Controllers was helping to create accessible equipment for disabled individuals. After several months of discussing my needs, they devised a DualShock 4 with two buttons on the outer sides of the controller handles. And, for several years, this controller was the only way I could play my PlayStation 4. Even with accessibility features in some games, they were all dependent on the device I was using.

Top left: PlayStation Access Controller with one of three joystick options.
Top right: PlayStation Access Controller side view, showing its 3.5mm ports.

I completed numerous titles, like Kingdom Hearts 3, Child of Light, Injustice 2, and even Knack. And, even though my PlayStation became my second preferred system after my original home-modified Xbox, I still had the capability to play. That is, until 2020.

First-Party Accessibility

In 2020, developer Naughty Dog released The Last of Us Part 2. Not only did this sequel to the 2013 original continue the story of Ellie – a protagonist in the first game who is immune to becoming infected by a dehumanizing virus – but it also added approximately 70 accessibility features for an array of disabilities. Motor, audio and visual accessibility settings were included to create the most accessible game of that year, and it won numerous awards, including for innovation in accessibility at The Game Awards. Customizable subtitles, difficulty settings, fully remappable controls and even auto-pathing, which automatically keeps the player on the appropriate path to facilitate progression for blind and low-vision players, were all crucial options that helped advance gaming accessibility. Yet, for me, my disability had progressed to the point where even my custom DualShock 4 controller could no longer function in my hands. While everyone praised the game's innovation, I was left struggling to convey my disappointment to my gaming peers.

Approximately one year earlier, Microsoft had released the first piece of first-party accessible hardware in over 30 years of games console manufacturing. The Xbox Adaptive Controller (XAC) acts as a hub, with nineteen 3.5mm ports, equivalent to every input on a standard controller, as well as two 2.0 USB ports for joysticks. Ports allow players to connect external buttons, switches and joysticks, meaning they can interact with the game through actions. Equipped with software that enables complete button customization, disabled players can create a setup that is unique to their specific needs, regardless of the game and its accessibility offerings. Despite this immense improvement in accessible hardware, spending money on an old technology – the Xbox One – so close to the end of its lifecycle was not worth it for me, but for the first time in my life, I had the power of choice.

I was able to fully test the XAC Series X during its initial launch in 2020. However, at this point Sony had yet to release its own accessible PlayStation controller, forcing me to return to Microsoft's Xbox game systems. And, while I was sad to abandon my previous generation's library of games because of system exclusivity, I was thankful that I still had the choice to play a console. My setup was equipped with switches and buttons from the Logitech G Adaptive Hardware Kit, a standard Xbox Series X controller and several switches and sticks from Warfighter Engaged, a nonprofit dedicated to creating accessible plug-ins for hardware. For the first time since I left my Xbox 360 behind, I was playing some of my favourite games, like Gears of War, Street Fighter and Octopath Traveler. More importantly, I had the confidence to try new games despite the progression of my disability. If I was unable to properly reach a button, I could just shift it to a closer position. Conversely, if my hands grew tired after extensive gaming sessions, I could switch the buttons to a different hand. More importantly, I did not need to rely on outside assistance to create my perfect setup. Once I purchased the necessary equipment, I could customize the layout within minutes.

Until December 2023, the XAC was my primary first-party device. However, that year Sony PlayStation released their own accessible controller to meet the needs of disabled players on the platform. The Access Controller comes equipped with nine buttons, 19 button caps which change the shape and size of the button, three joystick sizes, four 3.5mm AUX ports for extra buttons, switches or joysticks, and software settings that allow players to customize the inputs and their subsequent functions. But, unlike the XAC, the Access Controller is more akin to a standard controller, rather than a fully customized hub. Where the XAC offers complete freedom, albeit at the cost of table space and a higher price, for every switch, joystick and button, the Access Controller is a mostly complete device. Unfortunately, to receive the same button options as a standard Sony PlayStation DualSense controller, disabled players do need to purchase two controllers. Regardless of these differences and discrepancies,

with the industry offering two pieces of hardware that are fully supported by prominent industry leaders, disabled individuals have more choice and freedom to choose their preferred platform without fear of inaccessible hardware.

What's Next for the Industry?

Unfortunately, even with the release of the XAC and Access Controller, the needs of the disabled community are still not properly met. Arguably, the biggest issue with first-party accessible hardware is the cost. An XAC without any buttons, switches or joysticks costs in the region of $100. Since the device offers no peripherals in the box, disabled players are required to purchase extras to make a functional controller. Personally, my XAC setup totals approximately $400; this is $100 less than the Xbox Series X, and $100 more than the Xbox Series S. For disabled individuals on fixed incomes, a complete gaming setup – console, XAC, online membership and games – can come to well over $1000 if bought new. And, for a company whose tagline is 'When Everyone Plays, We All Win', the biggest barrier to Microsoft's accessible hardware is undoubtably the cost.

Sony PlayStation and their Access Controller fair marginally better, with one controller costing $90. However, as mentioned previously, two are required to offer the same buttons as a DualSense. Even with four extra ports, a second controller is needed.

Disabled players can expect to spend approximately $800 (over £600) for an entire PlayStation setup – two Access Controllers, a console, membership and games. While accessible hardware is meant to last across system generations, the initial set up cost can act as a barrier for many.

Beyond the issue of cost, disabled players continually push for hardware that is usable across different systems. Currently, the XAC and Access Controller are only operational on Xbox systems, PlayStation 5 systems and Windows-based computers, though the XAC is, for the time being, the only device that can fully function on a PC. If a disabled individual struggles to operate either of the controllers for their respective consoles, they are unable to switch devices. And, until recently, third-party adapters – USB-based devices that can be plugged into a system to override mandated hardware programming – were functional, that is until both Microsoft and PlayStation banned their use. These restrictions force disabled players to purchase first-party equipment for each system, while simultaneously losing thousands in now useless custom-created hardware.

While these examples are extreme cases, disabled players are constantly lobbying for more hardware options for current market offerings. More buttons, switches, joysticks, sizes, and even different colour schemes, are all requests that are regularly discussed on social media platforms. Disabled individuals are

rightfully pushing for more creativity and customization with their hardware, allowing them to confidently and comfortably play new games.

Even though companies are offering improved devices, their shortcomings are noticeable. Disabled players are forced to use creativity to design accessible controllers. From homemade modifications like my popsicle stick, to mouldable products like Sugru, or even 3D-printed objects to elevate sticks or make buttons easier to press, disabled ingenuity is at its best when we have no other choice but to adapt. Through sharing these modifications with each other, we demonstrate our sense of community, our resolve to belong in this industry and, above all, our love of gaming.

Above: Videogame tester Martin Shane uses a customized Playstation Access Controller layout and setup at the Sony headquarters.

How to Design a Font

Interview between Conor Foran and Natalie Kane

Dysfluent is a project led by Conor Foran that uses graphic design to represent how people who stammer speak. As part of this project, Conor created Dysfluent Mono, a typeface that repeats or stretches letterforms, giving stammering its own visual identity. The next interview is set in this typeface, and explores what it means for graphic design to represent or not represent your community. It expands upon some of Foran's other graphic explorations, delving further into what it means to have Stammering Pride. The following interview has been typset in Dysfluent Mono by Conor Foran.

Natalie: Can you tell us how Dysfluent Mono came about? It was quite a personal project and became much more of a community in the end?

Conor: Yeah, so it started back in 2017 as a university project that was born out of kind of a lot of pain and frustration that I was experiencing at the time with my stammer and the course I was doing – visual «c-«c-communication at NCAD (National College of Art and Design) in Dublin. At the time that was a course that was very much based on typography and print, so it felt kind of natural to maybe explore this part of me through typography. And I think it was a really exposing thing, I think – looking back I didn't really know what I was doing in the moment but like I was sh-⊜ltharing all these kind of stories and things with my friends and my tutors about stammering so that was really interesting. And I think that openness is something that I that I that I sort of practise now and I think that's why maybe it's it's been embraced by the stammering «c-c-community as well.

Natalie: Can you talk a bit more about the research that led you to it at university, as it has taken you to quite a particular place now? It seems like quite an iterative research project?

Conor: So the the research really began with myself. I think looking back it was   it had like   it had like an   it had like an auto-   ⊜thnographic approach I suppose. But I just didn't really realize that at the time because I was just ex- ex- ex-   ex-exploring my own lived lived experience because I didn't   know anyone else who stammered at the time and I think, back then, I didn't even like really understand stammering as a disability   ◯r a communication difference. I saw it as a speech impediment, which a lot of the world still understands it it as such. I saw it as a problem within me – in like the   in like the me in like the med-   the med-   the medical model kind of lens – but I think that's very different from now. I definitely see it   jiin a more social model lens and that definitely guides the current work that I do. In terms of the research visually, I remember looking a lot at resources that speech and language

therapists would use, like   the international ɾɾpʰth-   phonetic
alphabet,   which in itself is a really interesting attempt to apply
cataloguing to every single sound that can be made by the human mouth
and I found that really fascinating. I felt like it goes really far
kind of into being a code – that it's not really accessible, that you
actually can't really read it unless you really know wwh- wwłłhat these
letterforms mean. So in terms of the the ɾɾproduction of Dysfluent
Mono, I didn't want to go into that inaccessible realm and instead I
was looking at the work of 1920s łłDadaists who were making work with
concrete poetry and sound poems and I found that really interesting.
Tłłhey were really pushing the boundaries of ⊂f what expressive
typography can be and how łłtypography and sound can relate to each
other. In particular I remember this sound poem by   Marinetti
called 'Z-   Zang Tumb Tumb' and I think actually that's over 100
years old now but it ꞁꞁit it actually feels quite quite contemporary
łłlike like like in its execution. And that kind of work is extremely
expressive, so Dys- Dysfluent Dys- Dys- Dysfluent Mono is in ꞁꞁin in
between the concrete poetry and the kind of m⊜- the me-mechanical
formality of the of the international phon-ɾɾpłłhon-phonetic alphabet.

Natalie: I'm really interested in the tension between access and
experimentation within this kind of work. Could you talk a bit more
about that and explore that balance?

Conor: I think a lot of it has to do with how dysfluency can be
visualized itself. I think I think typography can only ever be
representational. I don't think the typeface is attempting to   łłli-
łłto   literally sound the stammer on on paper – it's kind of
impossible. I think stammering is so variable and it's so different
to to each person and I think there is there is a bit of tension there
between Dysfluent Mono almost being like a universal representation of
what stammering is and, in a way, that kind of ⸦⸦eels at odds with the
stammering experience because it's so different to each person. But I
think what Dysfluent Mono is trying to do is not replicate the stammer
but rather it is saying your stammering voice is is is unique but it
doesn't mean that your stammering experience needs to be a lonely one.

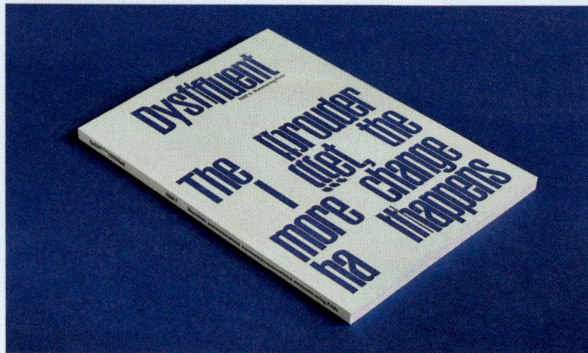
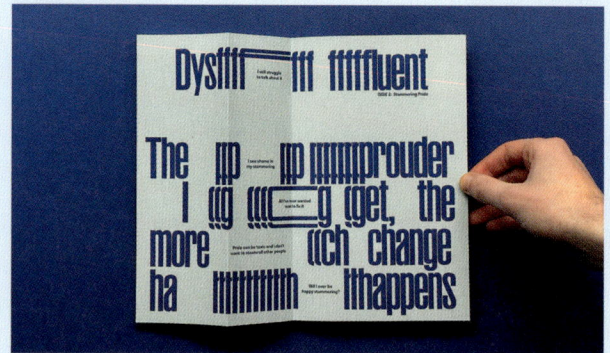

I almost see Dysfluent Mono as almost being a symbol or a badge or a crest of the stammering experience.

Natalie: I was wondering if you could talk a bit more about the font itself and the particular layout elements you've chosen?

Conor: The typeface is based on the three forms of stammering, so there's the prolongations, the repetitions and the blocks. It's also in in a «a mono-spaced font, which means that each letter is the same width. I did I did this strategically because it means that then all the stammering characters ⊐re in multiples of three and that and and like   and like as a system made it easier to design. What I think conceptually Dysfluent is at odds with is the unpredictability of stammering. It's kind of funny that that that that the font does feel quite mechanical in a way, but yet stammering is not that – but that's actually something ʈʈʈʈʈhat I explore in other parts of my work as well. I don't think the font can express all those facets of of ⊆tammering.

A lot of the stuff that we're talking about now, a lot of the stuff that that it it has achieved or maybe expresses, they they were not part of my intention, it it it just so happened the work does that by itself. I think that happens with with w   work too. I think at the time that I was just doing work and not really knowing where that was going to go or what it was going to say.

Natalie: Do you think that's because you chose print as a medium?

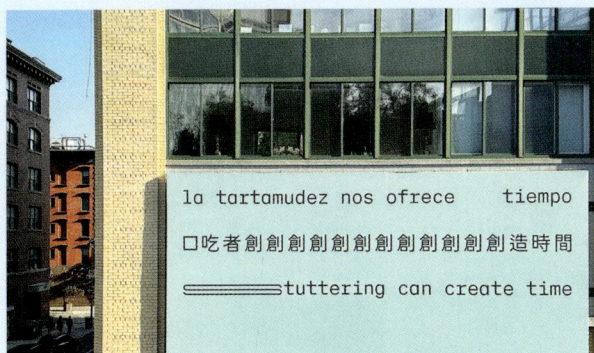

Conor: I think I think maybe it helped that there was that this was a first in the stammering ‹‹community, where I see now a]]lot of typography and fonts and branding of charities that that will use the same aesthetic as what I've developed, so I'm really conscious of that. I think maybe because it was a thing that people who stammer and speech and language therapists had never seen before, but maybe that's why it got a lot of traction maybe.

Natalie: Maybe it's a case of the community does it first and then the non-disabled community reacts because they're like actually this is what people have been asking for? In work such as your 2024 commission for the Biennial exhibition at the Whitney Museum of American Art (see above left), I've seen you explore speech as being not broken but created, and how those who stammer create space and time. It's an interesting and important reframing, and I'd love you to speak a bit more about that.

Conor: I think this idea of stammering ‹‹creating time and also sound ⌐orming over time was an idea that really guided the the making of the typeface and and the entire project really in terms of the flag, in terms of the magazine. And I think at the time   when the font was being made when I was researching the visual culture of stammering — a lot of it was like the branding for for therapists and charities, and a lot of it was words being broken and splintered and ⌐ragmented and weird-looking speech bubbles and mouths. I was like, 'There has to be a different way of expressing this that doesn't feel so damaging to our iiidentity.' I think I think looking back actually that was a 'stammering pride' approach but even at the time stammering pride wasn't like like even an idea back then but it's nice, looking back, that it has been guiding it the whole time. I think in terms of how ttthat informed the making of the typeface then, particularly the repetition of characters - a lot of those are kind of inspired by how the ttthe phases of the moon works, almost. There's like a bit of it that's visible, then a bit more, then a bit more, then a bit more and I think that just shows a kind of the   gradual experience of hearing a ww- a word or maybe a sound forming, essentially.

Natalie: I hadn't thought about it like that, in the ways that things ebb and flow, associating it to a natural process rather than seeing it as something disjointed or lacking - it's less of a deficit-based approach. You've talked about the flag (see p. 44) and stammering pride because, out of the personal, this community has developed. Do you see this as a protest? Is there a political relationship to it that you feel?

Conor: II think actually a lot of the ideas of stammering pride feel extremely radical, especially in the stammering   ⟪c-   community. They are inherently political - I think that's it's it's it's really understanding stammering as part of the disability and and neurodiversity paradigm. It's all in an effort to change perceptions and ttto to like like like instiga- ttto instigate social change. I think that has come about because I don't see stammering as a medical thing, needing it to be fixed, but rather a social thing that should be embraced. I think that's how the flag came about, too, because up until that point the only way that maybe stammering was being represented was by a ribbon. A ribbon is a mmmedical way of representing an experience or a condition and we said, 'If it's going to be a political movement, then then wwe need a flag.'

Natalie: A lot of your work is about advocacy and representation then, for yourself but also representing others? The Dysfluent publication is very unusual in that you are trying to represent something that is often erased or smoothed out. I use 'erased' in quite a politicized way, because people with stammers or lisps, for example, are often edited out or erased in text. How have you found trying to represent others through a typeface?

Conor: This is such a good question. It really makes me think! I think because the whole thing began wwith me back in college wanting to just try to express   my own voice, so so ⹀o then for that same piece of work to go on to represent like stammering people's voices – I didn't really intend – but I mean I'm so happy that that happened. And with a lot of people   who stammer, it's their choice to kind of see their own stammer in that, as well. I'm not gonna force that onto them. If the font doesn't represent the way they speak then that's totally fine too, but I think it's it's kind of linked to what I was saying earlier about what the font is specifically trying to do, which is not replicating the actual ⹀auditory experience of stammering, because that's actually impossible. It's just trying to say to the world that we're here, and this is a part of how we sound. I think also, on a deeper level, what I'd want people to take away from Dysfluent Mono and how it's being used in the magazine, is is is is the primacy of ⹀fluency – how, in in in day-to-day life, language is is is conventionally represented in typography. It's quite conventional and homogenous and that makes sense because it's a system that we all must understand. But for me it feels at odds with the experience of being a disabled person, or the experience of being a person who stammers. That language is so part of who I am, the way I speak – but we live in a hyper-fast, hyper-efficient world, one that demands us to be on time and do things in a certain way. Dysfluent Mono, just for those few moments that people read the magazine, I hope that it would make them think about language and «communication a bit differently.

Natalie: I really like the idea that you're trying to add to a politics of thinking around speech and language that hasn't really been explored. How important is it to reflect how someone speaks, for instance, in a landscape of technology like auto-captions and other things that don't accommodate different ways of speaking?

Conor: It's something that I think about a lot, but I don't know the answer to. I don't think a lot of people do because because because cause it's happening in real time and so quickly. When you talk about like like auto-captions, I don't think we know how that's going to impact people's sense of self ⊔ntil much later and especially as the world like interacts with   audio-command devices more and more, like that's that that is a huge discussion point in the stammering community as well. I think, though, Dysfluent is really trying to just be an advocate for stammering pride and ownership of voice, in all of the outputs that it makes. I think the erasure and minimization of stammering voices has been happening forever really, so the fact that it's like like like in a technological context … so I think as long as we keep an eye on what's happening and maybe we can like pee- ʀpeek our heads out and be like, 'That doesn't feel right!' then I think maybe that's the way forward. I think I think, though, there's already apps, and even speech and language therapists that work to 'fix' the stammer, and there are even fictional characters who have overcome their stammers, so these things are are happening all the time. I think I think though I ʈthink I think the more work that I do on this, in terms of visibility, I think all those cases of of erasure like actually kind of actually str-   they actually str-   they actually str-   strengthen and make a case for projects like Dysfluent. Because I think there's an there's there's an there's an ⊐⊔thentic policy to the work that I do — as long as I can continue that, I hope that that will be seen by people. I suppose time will tell!

Natalie: The Whitney billboard (see p. 39) had an unbelievable amount of visibility in terms of the different ranges of languages that you chose to work with. How did you find working with two languages that weren't your own?

Conor: So in in the collective that made the billboard, that «c-c-collective is called People Who Stutter Create, and so that was me, JJJJJerome Ellis, Jia Bin, Delicia Daniels and Kristel Ku-Kubart. So the act⊔al languages on the billboards were — first they were Spanish on the top, then Chinese and then English and ⊐ia, who is part of the collective, she is from China so we we had access there of course to to how the statement can be translated. Then we had some contacts who speak Spanish who stammered too. We rel- we relied on the ꞔcommunity ᵗtt-to help us there. I think working on the billboard was so interesting from a ꞁllanguage point of view because I think a lot of the work in the stammering community around stammering pride and these ideas is mainly just in the in the English-speaking world – so especially with this billboard being in New York, which is such a global ꞔcity, we really wanted it to speak to other languages. I think they are the three main languages apparently – so, in terms of the design of that, though, that was really interesting too because of Spanish being a language that that uses Roman characters. That works in the same way as the English version of Dysfluent Mono in terms of how things are repeated and elongated, but Chinese was interesting because we we chose to repeat characters there – but there's a long a ꞁllong discussion around how that even works like ꞊semantically and linguistically because, obviously, that language works so differently from from English and Spanish. Fortunately, the concept of of of of repeating the actual ideograms – that worked.

Natalie: Your practice is rooted in mass media and I'm interested in why you've chosen specific things, like flags and other mass-media graphics, for something that's so individual?

Conor: I really believe in the power of display and publication – I think especially being a graphic designer, I think there's so much power in things being shared en masse. There's a lot of work in the stammering community – it might be event- or or ꞔconference-led, or something where you must be there in person, and then it's done and that knowledge is kind of is is is like only available to the people that like attended those in person. I really want to make things that can be shared and seen all over the world because I think these ideas deserve to be seen by people who wwho stammer in the UK, in Ireland, ꞁꞁin India, in Brazil in loads of different countries.

Natalie: What do you have when you're first coming to terms with this?

What is the first interaction that you see – is it a doctor's office or is it a billboard outside the Whitney?

Conor: When I was growing up, I went to speech and language therapy a handful of times but but my exposure to stammering was like the film The King's Speech (2010), and like that was it. I generally didn't see it anywhere and that's the same as a lot of ɡɡpeople who stammer. It's mainly because we don't want to see stammering. It's only been in recent years that I'm I'm OK ɫtheairing other people stammer. It really takes a long time to deconstruct that and I think for things like the magazine and flag and other amazing ꜱtammering projects in the community but I think it's really important that they exist outside of the clinical spaces because it just shows that you aren't a test ꜱubject, that that that these things can be fun and beautiful.

Natalie: What are the things that you are keen to do next for this project? What do you think that you haven't achieved that you'd like to?

Conor: So, recently I was at the W the Whitney performing with a

collective and that was the first time that I was writing poetry about stammering, and it was kind of a bit of performance performance performance ⊜rt as well. And I really enjoyed that because it's the first time that, since ⊜ince making the first version of the font, that I started actually exploring my own experience of stammering. I've never actually shared my own stories and ideas. It's always been about other people who stammer and so I'm excited about about this next step. I'll still make a new like issue of the mag-magazine and do collaborations but I really want to to cont- to contri to contribute my own personal experience of stammering. I feel so lucky like with this project. It's like at any given moment I've got a ⊜ubject matter that I can tap into to express myself and make whatever ⊥ want, and it's given me so much personally and professionally, like personally I feel so empowered in my in my iii-in my stammering and di⊜abled identity, I've made such ammm- ammmmmmazing stammering friends. I've I've I've met some incredible people. Professionally, I I I get amazing opportunities to make mmmore art and more things, so it's really it's such a ⟨⟨generative experience that I think that I'm so happy that I leaned into it.

How to Design a Font

Interview between Natalie Kane and Emily Sara

504 font, created in 2023 by Emily Sara, is inspired by the events of the Section 504 sit-ins for disability rights that occurred across the USA in 1977. Each letter was pulled from posters and placards held by protesters, making up a typography which is 'purposely non-linear, purposely a mess', a living breathing record of an important moment in disability history.

Note from the artist:
'Only ABCDEFGHIJKLMNOPQRSTUVW♥YZ and 504 and ! are available. Z is an image of activist Judith Heumann, who died in 2023 but who continues to live on through the protests and the innate fiery nature of our crippled community.

A B C D E F
G H ▲ J K L M
N ◉ P Q ⚡ S T U
V W ♥ Y
5 ♿ 4 ! ! !

Natalie: Could you talk about the origins of the 504 Font and why you wanted to create it? I know a lot of your work comes from a personal place, as a Disabled designer, and I'd love to hear about the origins of the font itself.

Emily Sara: The 504 Font is a design I created that, much like my other work, stems from my history as an educator and from being a Disabled and neurodivergent student and, more recently, an artist and designer. My own practice is partly based on promoting the work or the history of other Disabled (including neurodivergent) individuals. I especially feel it's important to highlight disabled history since we typically don't learn about it in our more formal curricula. So much of how I've taught over the years is reflected in what I wanted, or needed, as a student and as a human in general. I think it's important to know your history and community in all facets of life. Part of my disability-related access started when I was in grade school. In fourth grade, here in the USA, my mom started a programme with several other moms to introduce students to talking about disabilities and also to listen to the community. I was in public school so it was basically all volunteer work. One time a blind woman came in and talked to us about what her everyday experiences were like. I distinctly remember a story about how she had trouble with her bank because they required a driver's license as proof of identity. She was talking to us about how ridiculous it was that they were so adamant about that specific

documentation, because she was blind and her service dog obviously couldn't drive. As simple as it was, it was pretty revolutionary that we just took time to sit and listen and talk with each other and with people about their own disability-related experiences.

I'm an ADA baby, meaning I'm part of the generation born around the Americans with Disabilities Act (ADA) that was implemented in 1990 in the USA. But, before that, Section 504 of the Rehabilitation Act of 1973 was really the first major federal law that prohibited discrimination against people with disabilities. It recognized disability as a protected civil right in the USA. A lot of the time when we talk about the civil rights movement in the USA and the Civil Rights Act of 1964, people are still largely unaware of the fact that it didn't include the disabled. Then, in April 1977, about three years and six months after these laws were established, people began protesting that the US government wasn't enforcing Section 504. So disabled individuals, with support from groups like the Black Panthers, took this into their own hands and started a highly organized campaign of sit-ins of government buildings across the country.

I think it's critical to recognize that it wasn't just the occupation of the Health, Education and Welfare (HEW) building in San Francisco, which was the sit-in that held out the longest – a total of 28 days. Protestors also organized occupations in Boston, Seattle, New York, Atlanta, Philadelphia, Chicago, Dallas, Denver and Washington DC. It was all organized amongst disabled individuals at a time when we didn't have cell phones or social media ... I think it's also important to note that when we talk about sit-ins they might seem pretty straightforward – but when you're disabled this is actually extremely dangerous. If you rely on medications or get pressure sores easily or need sterile equipment for catheters or open wounds as an example – not being in your regular environment without your regular support can be a major risk. The people that participated in these sit-ins put their lives on the line.

I built the 504 Font by accessing all the images of the 504 protests that I could from the internet. I gleaned each individual letter from those protest posters. I had to increase the contrast

and basically simplify the shapes from a photo representation into an illustration. Then I organized them into a very straightforward software that builds the font – much of this font-building software is available online for free. So, really, anyone can do this. When I published it, I emphasized that I was taking major inspiration from artist and writer Be Oakley, who founded the publishing and programming initiative GenderFail. Be took this approach with queer protests.

Opposite: Judith Heumann joining a San Francisco protest over housing discrimination, 1977
Above: Capitol City Crawl, led by Jennifer Keelan (left), 12 March 1990, Washington, DC

Natalie: The 504 Font comes from historical images of the protests, including one of notable disability activist Judith Heumann whose representation serves as the letter 'Z'. What else went into the process of researching more about this time, and then releasing the font itself?

Emily Sara: I think a lot of my research over the years stems from just wanting to know more about the individuals who were the change-makers in disability history. Like I mentioned before, this isn't typically taught in our grade-school curriculum or even in higher education. Not just the USA either – we have global disability history that is being lost because we aren't collectively preserving it or elevating the importance of it. That's a major disservice to all our communities unfortunately, since no one is exempt from disability. From what I see in major media outlets, we don't have a lot of support around disability narratives outside what we call 'inspiration porn', either. So what we find is that even the more recent disability-related events and the people that make them happen are just not well known. Individuals like Brad Lomax, Ed Roberts, Fannie Lou Hamer, Lois Curtis and Elaine Wilson – the list is endless.

I'm always thinking about how the context of something like our history or our stories as humans are actually quite disjointed. This disjointedness is something I embrace with my work and I inject it into my art regularly now.

When you are neurodivergent and disabled you don't have the same hours in a day or the same bandwidth as the non-disabled. Your 'plan' or schedule is very disrupted by illness, chronic pain, inaccessible spaces, ableism and so forth. Things are out of balance; they are often clunky and they don't follow the rules. The concept of 'normal' doesn't exist when you're disabled. With the 504 Font, it's purposely very messy and doesn't have the normal rhythm of a regular font that comes out of a typical type foundry. It's probably very irritating to many graphic designers to be honest – and that's very intentional.

Since I couldn't find a letter Z in my research, and all of this already didn't follow the rules of a 'normal' font, I decided to memorialize Judy Heumann who was highly instrumental in the 504 protests and who unexpectedly passed away in 2023. I think of the 504 Font as a protest against the neglect of our disabled history.

Natalie: This font is an archive of history and archive of disabled people's political lives. You might not see what people are doing with it in the same way as a traditional archive, and I think there's something in that – to bear witness with artefacts like this which lean on graphic design and print, perhaps, as a medium. What does it mean for you to do something that's so historically positioned and for you to hold a community in this way?

Emily Sara: I definitely did think about

how individuals are downloading this font and may not even necessarily be using it. There's such a comfort in knowing that this is their history, and that there is something they can just hold on to and love and be a part of. It's the reclaiming – as a protest against the neglect of our history. I constantly think about the dissemination of work by disabled artists and with this, I really believe in supporting free education as much as possible, by and for our community. *Cripple*, the publishing initiative I founded, exists online as a multifaceted archive – one that provides extensive resources and support.

I love that someone could download the 504 Font and be seeking information about disability with *cripple* because they are questioning their own identity around disability. I recognize that not everyone can live out loud about their disability, especially if you are multiply marginalized. Being disabled and also being perceived as disabled in many ways is still quite dangerous, unfortunately. We see instances throughout history, and certainly in a contemporary sense as well, where disability is weaponized. For instance, during the civil rights era here in the USA and during a time of 'deinstitutionalization' – moving away from long-stay psychiatric hospitals towards community health services – schizophrenia was being added to the charge sheets of Black individuals who participated in various civil rights protests. So schizophrenia was used as a weapon of control – to label

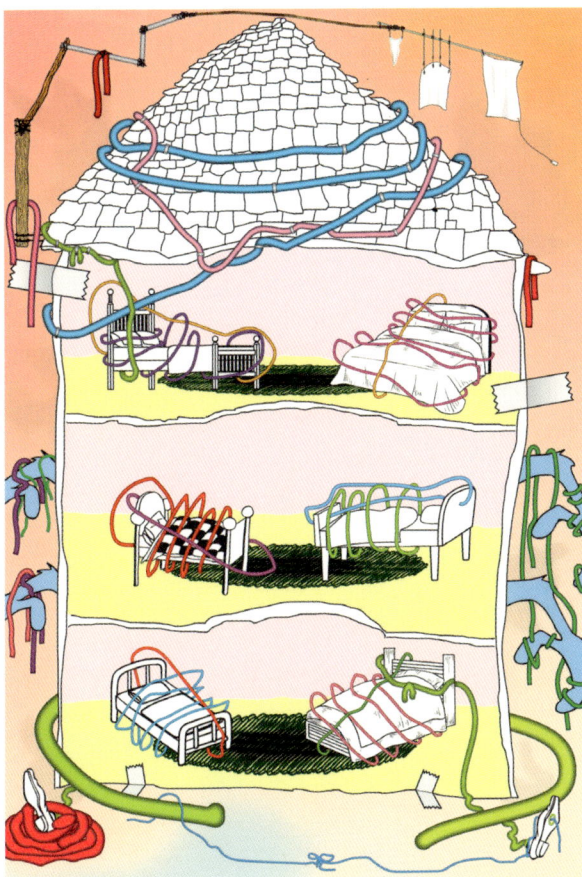

Black protestors as dangerous and to dehumanize them and remove their rights under the pretext of disability.

So, again, I wish we lived in a world where everyone could openly support their disability as an identity and a label – but that's not entirely where we are at the moment. I think that it is critical to support someone's level of comfortability or safety as well. I think that something like the 504 Font can

Above: Emily Sara, *A pink house for me and my friends*, inkjet print, 2023

really participate in that individual growth around questioning and identity – so maybe they make a card or a post on social media using the font and someone else has no idea of the context, but they know. If it's the case that you can't live out loud or you're learning about disability and your own history, that can be everything – to just have community and to not feel so lost in a world that was built for the non-disabled.

Natalie: You have talked quite a lot about mess in your work and used words such as 'mess' or 'dishevelled' to describe it. I don't know whether you use them in the same breath as the term 'disability aesthetics', and whether you could just define for me what you understand to be disability aesthetics, but I'd love to hear more about these ideas.

Emily Sara: Thank you – I'm so glad you brought that up! Well, I'll start by saying there's a big issue when you're disabled and an artist, especially when you're developing your practice and you haven't gotten a ton of recognition yet. You make very intentional decisions and people will have no hesitation in making comments about a part of your work being wrong. It stems from the infantilization that happens when you're disabled. Dehumanization leads to this infantilization – even, at times, from people who think they are being allies to the disabled. A form of commentary happens: people will inform you that things you do are plainly incorrect, even if they are purposeful, specific artistic or design-based choices.

This is because they think that you don't know what you're doing. I recognize that my whole life and the lives of other disabled and neurodivergent individuals are outside the spectrum of what we might call 'normal' – but that doesn't mean that our decisions or our lives are innately wrong.

For many years I have felt the need to literally say with my art or with my drawings, 'This is intentional!' This could show up as quick movements or by using a stereotypical form of tracing in Illustrator. Lines are purposely mismatched and at lower resolution at times; overly compressed and blurry spaces are introduced in sections of very large, high resolution and complex drawings. Or even using fonts that are highly accessible but which a seasoned designer in the industry would never dream of using. I just love all that stuff. Like, why not? That 'wrongness' is also highlighted in *Disability Aesthetics*, a book by Tobin Siebers published in 2010. I highly recommend it – it talks about how so much of modern and contemporary art is centred in this wrongness. It's a disabled perspective and aesthetic. Our bodies are not 'normal'. We are the antithesis of normal. How much of art, both modern and contemporary, is based in that antithesis as well? It turns out a lot, actually.

Even with the 504 Font itself, I did quick manoeuvres and left them how they were, whether it's 'visually appealing' or not. I think it's quite critical to have things 'in the wrong'. I've coined a theory called Stim Aesthetics (stim is short for 'self-stimulatory behaviour') which, I believe, is the next step beyond disability aesthetics because it platforms the neurodivergent perspective as well.

Natalie: There is such pressure for design work by disabled people to be only about access, with no space for experimentation. This is what I find really interesting about your work, and particularly the 504 font and the other graphic design work that you do. I've always thought about it in terms of 'anti-access', because anti-access doesn't mean it's not accessible – just like the antihero is not the villain but someone who's come to heroism in non-traditional ways. Anti-access, in work created by disabled people, might be understood to be about first innately understanding access itself and then subverting it. This could be using a neurodiverse-friendly colour palette to create something unexpected. How do we balance that tension, particularly as designers who want to investigate that space, considering the position that we come from.

Emily Sara: I love everything you just said and I do believe there is a certain pressure in regards to a certain type of access – and a void of experimentation that can stem from that. Almost no one brings this up about disabled art and it's wild to me that they don't. So, thank you for that. So much of my work is about experimentation. Many people give me pushback – 'Well, is this accessible?' –

so I'm always saying, 'Accessible to who, exactly?' We have different standards of access. We have laws in the USA – the ADA, or Americans with Disability Act – which have certainly grown over the years and are also, at the time of this writing, facing being dismantled by our current administration. Initially, when the ADA was signed into law in 1990, it was geared more towards access in physical space and then it eventually incorporated the public sphere of websites like it does today. The ADA provides specific standards, which are really great and it's certainly critical we uphold this support. I'm not denying that. But they provide only a certain amount of access and also for certain individuals. With my own art, I think about access in regard to, for example, neurodivergence and stimming. So, as an example again, I'll include over-whelming buzzing with strong colours and movement.

Natalie: I was wondering if you could speak a bit more about your wider publishing initiative *cripple* as I know it's another way for you to work through these ideas with others?

Emily Sara: Yes, *cripple* is absolutely a collaborative process. First, it's a living library with many arms – a non-linear archive of information and resources, and beyond. It also entirely depends on the work of others. In instances where I'm documenting someone's work or doing an interview or making a book, I'd say that experimentation is highly critical as well. I think, again, part of this

5 & 4

FONT

is subverting what we consider to be 'normal' with everything and certainly with what we consider as 'publishing'. But also with what we come to expect with disabled art and design.

In publishing, there's so much stress on rigid deadlines and getting things absolutely 100 per cent correct. So with *cripple*, I absolutely do not push that traditional narrative. Disabled bodies simply do not have the same timeline as non-disabled bodies. So if strict parameters and the exact same formula was given to each entity that is produced through cripple, a lot of this work would just never happen. And this is honestly one of the many reasons why we also don't see enough of this work out in the world.

I've witnessed it many times where someone who is disabled wants to write about something and the publisher will say, 'This isn't what we do,' and they pass on it. Disabled creatives also don't have the luxury of choosing from a variety of spaces that will support their work because we don't have many people higher up in the industry who also understand where we're coming from. I've seen some people passing on some truly brilliant work. And that's such a disservice to our society at large, if we lose this massive chunk of creativity in the world. So, it's really critical for me and for *cripple* to be highly flexible when and where needed. To be non-linear in all facets. To say, 'OK, if this is a book, if this is a documentary, if this is a sculpture – let's do it.' It's collectively

working, as part of my own art practice, to assist others in bringing to fruition their work, with their own access needs, with their own aesthetics and, ultimately, their own voice. That's what *cripple* is. My community's history is being lost or acutely neglected, and that can feel like a tidal wave at times. I just decided at one point in my life that this preserving, this support, this mutual-aid as art, is what I want to dedicate my everything towards, if that makes sense? I think it's important. It's my hope that others will too.

How to Design a Home

Natalie Kane interview with Christopher Laing and Jordan Whitewood-Neal

Deaf Architecture Front, founded by Christopher Laing, aims to support Deaf people wanting to get into architecture, consult on projects according to Deaf Space ideas and act as an open-source resource. Jordan Whitewood-Neal is a co-founder of Dis, a disability-led art and architecture research collective which argues for disabled and crip experience to be valued within our culture and environment. Dis also offers critical perspectives on transcultural experiences of debility. Dis's work is based on disability narratives and alternative approaches to pedagogy that work against racial, capitalist and ableist processes in the built environment. Fundamentally, they explore alternative ways of living, surviving and thriving.

Natalie: I put you together because I think you're both brilliant architectural minds, and I was hoping that we could have a conversation about the role of access in architecture and living, drawing on your combined expertise. So the first question is a really simple one: how do you build a house?

Christopher: How do you build a house? You say it's a simple question! I'd want the space to feel warm, with visual elements of the Deaf Space design philosophy included, but I don't want it to be obvious. I want it to be incorporated into a beautiful aesthetic design, and that would be the perfect house for me – one that combined aesthetic and Deaf Space elements.

Jordan: So I took it in a more metaphorical way, maybe. And that was maybe even more complicated, because the question to me of how you build a home – I think it's interesting because how often do we, as disabled people, get a chance to actually build a home? Because we often have to rely on spaces which are already built and already inadequate. And the agency to actually build your own space can be quite limited. Therefore the idea of actually being able to build a home is quite an exciting one – to imagine the space in the same way that Chris is proposing, that it is built around your own pragmatic/aesthetic/ethical ideals, which I really like. I think it's very difficult to actually imagine the ideal home, let alone build it. So yeah, I think maybe we start there? How do we even imagine a home, Chris?

Christopher: I completely agree with that, Jordan. I feel that most of us, especially within the Deaf community, we're so attuned to fitting in with hearing design or always adapting to fit into the spaces that don't work for us. So, actually, having an opportunity to design in a way that would fit me, fit us, through our experience. What works? What doesn't work? What works well? And adjusting that. I think that would enable it to become your home more.

Natalie: How do we start to pull this design process apart, to open it up from a perspective of disabled architects or critics – people who obviously have a unique perspective?

Christopher: I think co-design and collaboration through design processes, incorporating different perspectives throughout, is a way to start creating that. You know, what are the benefits and what are the negatives of each different perspective and view? And having that throughout, that co-creation throughout a process, I think would be the best way. There's not that much opportunity for that, and there are gaps for all people to be represented in these spaces – Deaf, disabled and neurodiverse people. And for that to happen regularly throughout the process, whether it be home design or specialist kitchens or whatever it is, creating resources for homes, or generally – we need specific case examples.

Following spread: The Black and White building, London, designed by Waugh Thistleton Architects

Clockwise from top left:
The Circulation Space at London College of Fashion, designed by Allies and Morrison; The Atrium Space at The Deaf Academy, designed by Stride Treglown; MAC Belfast, designed by Hall McKnight; A booth at The Black and White Building, designed by Waugh Thistleton Architects with interiors by Daytrip Studio; The Deaf Academy; standpoint view, London College of Fashion

Natalie: Why do you think there's been that gap? What do you need to happen at a pragmatic level and in more structural ways?

Christopher: I think the gap is there because the people leading these design processes – are they offering opportunities for workshops or forum spaces? Or opportunities for Deaf and disabled people to be involved in the design? Sometimes these buildings are done, and there are barriers, and there has been no opportunity for people who have to deal with these barriers to be involved with different experiences throughout that process. And so, that's a huge pragmatic thing – Deaf people as an example, being involved in the process. It needs inclusive design conversations – having consultations with people who represent these communities. And have the design changing and updating throughout the process to adapt to different needs. And the gap is opportunity and providing space for people to be involved. For me, as a Deaf person, the design process or consultation are not inclusive processes. They're not accessible, there are no interpreters at these consultations. Information is often written down, so there's no access to this. If there was a video in BSL (British Sign Language), or a forum space where I would be comfortable to provide my opinions, in my first language, with an interpreter there ... Opportunities like that are the pragmatic things that would help involve different communities.

Jordan: Yeah. I think, going back to the earlier question about how we critique, or how we initiate change, I think for Deaf, disabled and neurodivergent and the multiple different communities that we are talking about here, they have the potential to upend the way we think about how homes are structured, both socially and spatially. Which, as we know, have been formed by particular ideas of social reproduction, of politics, of work ... ideals that form the way that the home functions for people.

So I question the fundamentals of what a home is, what it provides, what it enables you to create – and I also think about where the boundaries of the home are. Is the neighbourhood part of the home? I think this is a particularly interesting question when you think about disability. Because, from a personal perspective, I sometimes felt a sense of isolation in the way that the home internalizes a lot of ideas of care, of self-preservation, and actually doesn't always enable you to reach out to your wider community.

There's a sense of being dispersed, and that sense of community can sometimes be difficult to formalize, and I think the way that homes are currently created contributes to that. So I would like to see more attention on housing models, and the way we live together, as a way to upend those deeper systemic issues that that homes currently reinforce.

Natalie: Yeah, it's a really good point – the idea of home expanding to mean community. How do you create a

community that enables Deaf, disabled and neurodivergent people to thrive? What does that look like? And how do you make sure that anti-racist sensibilities are also considered, and what other things are important to think about? What does a community look like that holds all of these things in balance?

Above: Samuel, a filmmaker, documented Chris's journey to becoming an architect as part of the Deaf Architecture Front (DAF) Launch.
Left: The DAF presentation showcased the event's significance, supported by the Deaf community and allies' applause.

Christopher: To my knowledge there isn't a really good example of Deaf Space in the UK. A building would need to evidence all the Deaf Space elements, using reflection, peripheral sight lines, vibration and transparency. As there isn't one example of best practice, maybe four buildings that, if combined, would be. I'll choose a timber office building by Fora Space, in London, the Deaf Academy in Exmouth, Devon, the arts venue MAC Belfast and the London College of Fashion building designed by Allies and Morrison (see p.60).

I think it's difficult, it's hard. It really depends on the Deaf community, and people within the Deaf community have different needs. I think, for me, it's openness and transparency. Deaf Space is where you can feel safe, feel you've got that kind of visual perspective – you know what's going on in terms of the physical.

But also it's not having the power to make change – you know, regulations don't match people's needs necessarily, or our requirements. Things need to happen higher up to influence change and that's a huge barrier. You've got building regulations but there's not enough detail in there to match the needs of diverse communities. There's information missing. So how can we get higher up and integrate change from the top down?

Natalie: What is it about the current building regulations that fail? Can you give an example?

Christopher: There is a focus on hearing loops, and less provision for Deaf BSL natives who don't use hearing-aid

Above: The DisOrdinary Architecture Project and ReFabricate, *Seats at the Table* (2023), temporary intervention at Postman's Park, London

devices. Deaf Space elements are not in building design guidelines, and they need to be. For instance, take fire alarms. Are there guidelines to ensure that they are positioned in a place that is easily visible? That all alarms are sound and flash? On many occasions I have been present in a building when a fire-alarm test goes off and I have no idea as they are sound only. The building regulations fail as they don't match the needs of the Deaf community.

Natalie: It's marrying systemic and legislative change, but it's also behaviour and wider community change – between disabled and non-disabled communities – and how to match access at multiple levels. I mean, I always come back to this idea of access intimacy. Do you know what I mean by the concept? Writer and educator Mia Mingus (see p. 93) coined this phrase and concept. It's an elusive concept of someone just knowing your access needs, without it necessarily being explicitly political. Imagining that at a personal or community-wide level – I think that would be something to explore.

Christopher: Yeah, I think that kind of concept ... You know, when I think about Deaf Space, there's also another phrase 'Deaf Gain', which is that, actually, there are benefits to being Deaf and being Deaf can benefit the wider community at large. So why can't we integrate these into design, you know? Deaf Space elements can benefit not only the Deaf community, they can benefit everybody. And a diverse group of people.

Natalie: Can you give an example of Deaf Gain in architecture?

Christopher: Deaf Gain can benefit everyone: for example buildings that are designed with clear sightlines mean visitors can experience a space, seeing one another at distance and in proximity, and are able to communicate in BSL. In general, the Deaf community experiences Deaf Gain in a way that a non-Deaf person wouldn't.

Jordan: Something that I'm interested in because we wrote a brief about it for the London School of Architecture, is intergenerational housing. Both as a starting point to understand and critique, and as a starting model for how we think about the way that disabled communities in the broadest sense, including ageing, can come together in an interdependent community. And what we're currently looking at is how transcultural and transnational disability narratives are understood within those communities, as well. So even within a single country, there is no homogeneous cultural approach to how disability is understood, talked about, cared for, etc. We were looking at a site in Brent, in West London, which has a huge diaspora community, and the different ways that those communities actually engage with disability and centre projects and forms of care and infrastructures around that. There is a specific London-based group – the Asian Disabled People's Association in Britain – who have done a lot of work around care for disabled communities.

And that, to me, is key to developing new forms of living that bring those together. Also, what Chris was saying about Deaf Gain in terms of Deafness being able to provide more than just for a Deaf community – I think it's so important. It also speaks to the way that we can learn together. By being together you are learning from each other.

I'm thinking of the 504 sit-in in the USA in 1977 – the protest where signing was used as a form of covert communication between the protesters and the people outside as a way of getting round the police and getting around other forms of oppression at that site. I'm also really interested in how homes can take on a kind of pedagogical role in how we not just live together but actually learn from each other in the process of living.

Christopher: Yeah. I think it's also sad when you think about hearing design – it's only when people think, 'Oh gosh, I could become Deaf when I'm older. Oh, I need to take some action!' They're not thinking about us the Deaf community now, but thinking about changes and additions in the future when this happens to them. That's a huge kind of societal attitude.

Natalie: What do you think is a starting point to getting co-design underway?

Jordan: That's very funny – I had a very similar question for you! Yeah, I think this is where, again, it comes back to learning with each other. And, in terms of both language and general knowledge, and also communication, to design together I think we also need to get to know each other beyond that particular co-design space, so that we are a community before we come to that. I think that would strengthen the process itself.

Christopher: Yeah, I know, I hear you. I feel, pragmatically, we need funding, getting people together for research. And also mandatory regulations. Education through workplaces, through universities. And making policy and having co-design throughout the design process – that becoming compulsory.

Jordan: And a space to come together, as well. I think it would be amazing if we, as communities, had a space to actually come together to work on these things. And I think community infrastructure that enables that is very rare. It's a critical part of us being able to do that work. Finding those spaces, or finding ways to procure those spaces, is going to be really important. And that, in itself, becomes a home for something, right? Going back to your original question of how do you build a home? Maybe that is part of it.

Christopher: Just one final comment. In my office, we regularly have a Green Day that talks about climate and sustainability. But if there was something equivalent – workshops, education, discussions in favour of Deaf, disabled and neurodiverse spaces and how to implement change from co-design – that could then provide something tangible for education.

65

How to Design a Neighbourhood

Essay by Natalie Kane

How we do live together, and how do we ensure disabled people thrive? Block Party is a collaborative architecture and urban design project which takes on housing justice from a disability-first perspective, reimagining the future of a single block in Berkeley, California. Featuring tactile models and a wall-length mural filled with thought-provoking proposals built on years of disabled expertise, Block Party asks us to open up the city as a shared resource, rich with possibility.

TACTILE MAP

The tactile model was produced in direct collaboration with blind artist Georgina Kleege, using 3D printing and different material elements, with an accompanying audio description of a journey through the site and its different areas. Architectural exhibits can be highly visual, so this was an opportunity to engage with Block Party's architectural and urban strategies through a more experiential narrative engagement. Striped and striated textures denote newer structures, smooth tops are existing buildings and honeycombing details indicate new accessible walkways and property lines. Kleege, whose work expands the notion of what sensory experience can and should be, encouraged the team to use different materials. Softer, pliable rubbers were chosen for their more pleasurable qualities, with certain textures reminding Kleege during the design process of sex toys. Further textural patches were applied to the 3D-printed base to lead the bearer on a sensory journey through the neighbourhood.

The Block Party: From Independent Living to Disability Communalism project began in 2022 to offer a critique of existing housing stock and urban planning which all too often excludes disabled people and marginalized communities, as well as dividing communities across racial lines. This exploration was focused on one block in Prince Street in South Berkeley, California, a site of significant disability justice history.

Starting with a commissioned exhibition in New York at the Center for Architecture in 2022, the project pulled together a team of disabled and non-disabled collaborators in order to bring a wider disability critique of property[1] and the built environment. Architect Brett Snyder, architectural historian Irene Cheng and disabled designer and historian of architecture David Gissen initiated the project together with a team of student interns from UC Davis, California College of the Arts (CCA) and The New School Parsons.[2]

The project's name comes from an extension of the block party in the USA, where neighbours come together in communal spaces to socialize. It felt natural, therefore, that this project was a collaboration across many disciplines and many histories, inviting other practitioners to imagine futures together. It was important to the team for disabled people not to be seen as the hired occasional consultants in the room, but to be the ones leading and authoring the discussions. Disabled

artists Georgina Kleege and Chip Lord and dancer Jerron Herman were subsequently invited to bring their experience of disability to the project as equal collaborators, bringing plurality to the ways in which space could be understood. Herman, in talking about his involvement, suggests that artists perform a 'radical act of changing what that building had in mind to be'.[3]

From a disability-first perspective, and for the team at Block Party, 'communal flourishing', as defined by Cheng, means not just meeting the minimum levels of access required by codes or regulations, but having a 'maximalist' approach to redesigning a community, including having many different community spaces, such as those for recreation and rest, that cater for multiple modes of access.[4] Beyond housing and basic resources, such communities achieve something significantly more enriched – enabling the arts and other activities of pleasure to be woven into the fabric of communities as they develop, creating the capacity for culture and creativity to emerge in abundance.

The thinking around access provision, from an infrastructure and urban-planning perspective, is often focused on compliance, but communities and researchers alike have worked to bring greater attention to access injustice through projects such as Block Party. Through mapping an area, such as a university campus, the project reveals and records errors as they appear to those who experience them. Often,

MODEL

Block Party aimed to develop the history of the Berkeley campus as a site with many layers of architectural history. Existing buildings are detailed in wooden blocks while new interventions are rendered in white, with magenta felt for new accessible pathways.

There is speculative reimagining laced throughout the model. It reintroduces objects of desire such as the therapy pool – otherwise known by disabled communities on Berkeley High campus as Berkeley Warm Pool, which was shut down in 2012 – but in new ways. The team also proposed new buildings to encourage communalism across some of the current property boundaries. Here, they are positioned in plain sight, showing how they transform the walkways into areas of shared space.

for disabled people, a form of design connoisseurship emerges for reading the environment through their own lived experience: I see this kerb in a way that you do not read that kerb; this tree-lined street means something different to my body than to yours. Codes, therefore, may fix some problems, by requiring a smattering of ramps to solve entryway problems, but may not address difficult terrain, or exhausting distances between spaces, or the need for shade or cover. Block Party encourages the subversion of city codes to encourage shared spaces and throughways, such as in The Meander [see right] which creates accessible walkways in the unused spaces between buildings. Neighbours are encouraged to pull down fences between their own private properties to create a larger 'shared yard', creating green spaces for wider enjoyment – a further strategy of 'commoning' that pushes the boundaries of regulations.

The choice of location for the Block Party project was no coincidence: beyond being familiar to several of those on the project (many of whom live or were born close by), Berkeley itself is also a place of deep historical importance for the disability community. Activists emerged there in the 1960s and 1970s at the University of California, Berkeley, because of the work of disability justice leader Ed Roberts (for whom one campus is named) – he was the first wheelchair user to attend the university, in 1962. Roberts and his peers protested for significant changes around the city of Berkeley and on the university

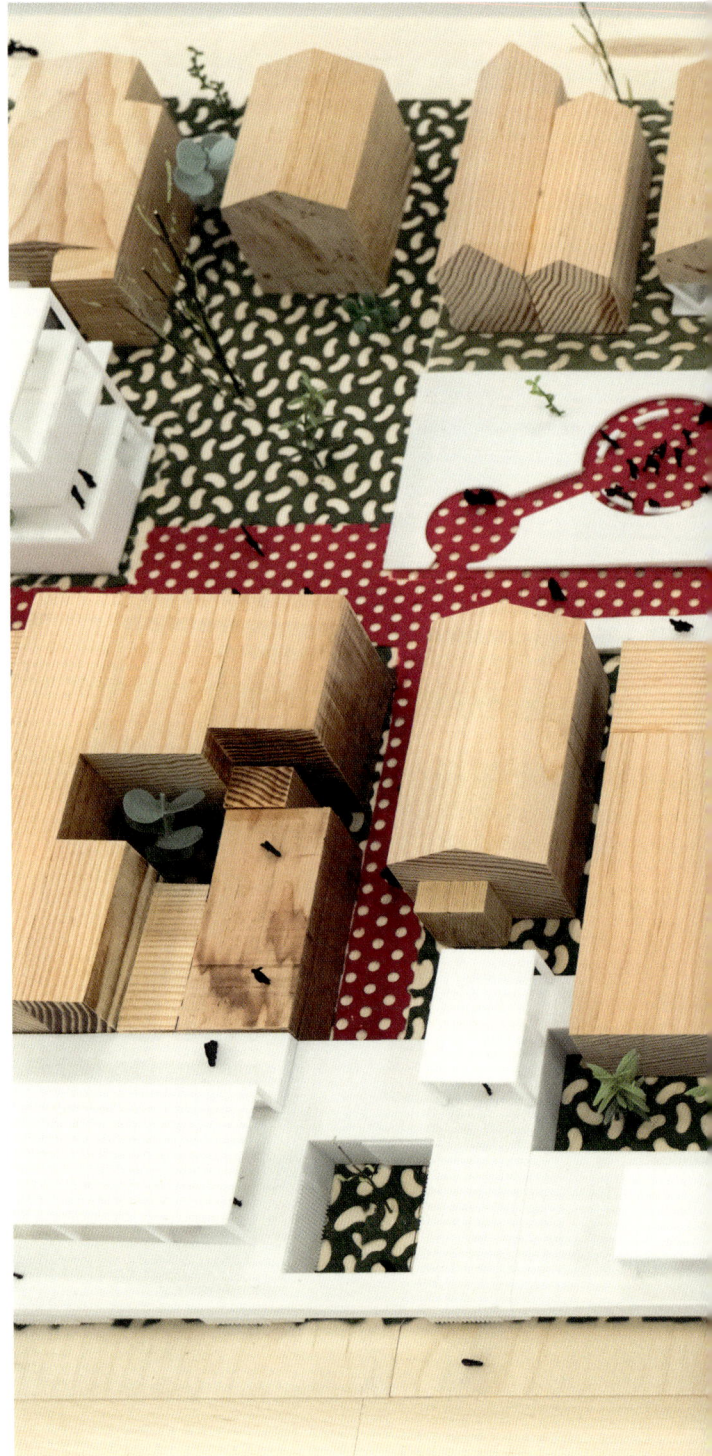

campus, including the first kerb cuts (ramps from pavement to road level), and led many others to demand change, including disability activist Judith Heumann. In 1972 Roberts, together with other disabled students, helped found the Berkeley Center for Independent Living (CIL) enabling disabled people to live together outside institutions. Its first site borders the Block Party project.

Berkeley was also central to the Section 504 sit-ins in April 1977. These demanded the implementation of the part of the Rehabilitation Act of 1973 that prohibited discrimination against disabled people by federally funded programmes. Although a nationwide event, the sit-ins reached their peak at the Department of Health, Education and Welfare (HEW) in nearby San Francisco. Organized out of the CIL with civil rights organization Disabled in Action, the sit-in was led by Heumann, Kitty Cone, Corbett O'Toole, Brad Lomax, Mary Jane Owen, Hale Zukas, Dennis Billups and countless others. The group occupied the HEW for 26 days with support from the Black Panthers, Gay Brothers and Sisters, Mission Rebels and church groups, forcing the clause to be enforced and setting further changing into motion.

Block Party aims to bring an intersectional disability critique to California's urban-planning history, which is rooted in racism and classism. Berkeley was the birthplace of single-family zoning, implemented first in the neighbourhood of Elmwood in 1916.

Single-family zoning is, simply put, a form of planning that restricts the building of housing to single-family detached homes. Exclusionary by design, zoning regulation encouraged a reduction in smaller, affordable housing and reduced any sense of community. Residents are far less likely to share resources if their sense of neighbourliness is physically reduced due to their relative spatial isolation. Many of these houses were also designed for non-disabled, car-owning families (with an emphasis on a very particular type of assumed nuclear family) and do not include adjustments such as lifts or ramps.

Elmwood's zoning originally prohibited people of colour from owning property in the neighbourhood and blocked the building of a Black-owned dancehall.[5] However, change does happen, albeit slowly: in February 2021, Governor Gavin Newsom signed California senate bills leading to the abolishment of single-family zoning in Berkeley and enabling development of affordable housing in the area. Block Party greeted the removal of this oppressive legislation as a point of creativity, future speculation and opportunity, though they stress that it must happen within an existing ecosystem of community adaptation.

Where Block Party worked with existing buildings and infrastructure at its original Prince Street site, there were now multiple proposed interventions in the wider San Francisco area that Gissen describes as 'scaffolds' to support activities that are already happening, reinforcing strategies that disabled residents have historically used to access Berkeley and the Bay Area. They include a lift and bridges that could serve as walkways for multiple properties, and the adaptive waterfront bike paths for the Bay Area Outreach and Recreation Program (BORP). Block Party is not trying to create anything new, but rather build on an existing conversation that would (in Cheng's words) flourish if properly enabled. Block Party explores what Cheng, Snyder and Gissen call 'disabled communalism' – how new collective spaces that prioritize access emerge from the sharing of space across boundaries, often by subverting private boundaries or city regulations.[6] Block Party aims, ultimately, to encourage spaces that give connection without obligation and access that feels part of the fabric of the environment.

Research for the Block Party project included a series of interviews with its own team as well as with disabled activists and residents in Berkeley, including Yomi Wrong and Ojan Mobedshahi of the East Bay Permanent Real Estate Cooperative. These revealed how the urban environment creates barriers and friction for disabled people – from cars being parked incorrectly to uneven and badly maintained sidewalks. The conversation also, though, steered towards moments of joy, highlighting projects that celebrated togetherness, collective ingenuity and fun. There was also a desire for a reconsideration of pace

with neighbourhoods designed for rest and proposals for paths that encourage slower movements through neighbourhoods. These, together with 'lazy rivers', shared desires for resource sharing and a move towards communal living. Voices thus become embedded within the landscape and an enveloping history of place evolves through a different and enlivened approach to access.

The first display of Block Party's work was for *Reset: Towards a New Commons*, an exhibition curated by Barry Bergdoll and Juliana Barton at the Center for Architecture in New York in 2022, which aimed to envision new dynamics of living and community. To ensure remote-viewing access for disabled and immunocompromised communities that would not be able to attend on site, a digital exhibition was also presented.

A CONSTELLATION OF EXPERIMENTAL BLOCKS

HASKELL MABEL MINI PARK

PRINCE STREET MINI PARK

INTRODUCTION

PEOPLE TOOK SLEDGEHAMMERS AND CREATED THEIR OWN CURB CUTS!

DISABILITY JUSTICE TODAY

Our project asks: Can we envision a multiracial disability community that addresses not only individual needs but also shared pleasures and "communal luxury"?

ZONING AND PROPERTY

The single-family configuration of many city blocks in Berkeley (and across the country) contributes to the scarcity of affordable housing, and discourages the sharing of resources.

THE PROBLEMS WITH SINGLE-FAMILY ZONING

Houses are designed for able-bodied, nuclear families with cars, and they rarely include ramps or elevators.

Things are changing though! In 2021, the Berkeley City Council voted to abolish single-family zoning in the city.

A NEW APPROACH TO ZONING

RAISED BASEMENT

GARAGE CONVERSION

BACKYARD COTTAGE

These changes, combined with other measures to promote housing affordability, will hopefully open the way to denser forms of housing, including backyard cottages, duplexes, and cohousing, that can welcome more diverse residents and ways of life.

THE PLEASURES OF MIXING

ENHANCE, DON'T DISPLACE

Could these new forms of denser housing be harnessed to support multiracial disability communities engaged in mutual aid and communal flourishing?

STRATEGIES OF COMMONING

GRAPHIC NOVEL

As a response to the interviews, a series of illustrated tableaux was commissioned, creating a graphic novel that provided both an historical context of the area and the future possibilities for the block. These were presented as a large mural (see below and overleaf), made tactile in places where pathways and thoroughfares were present.

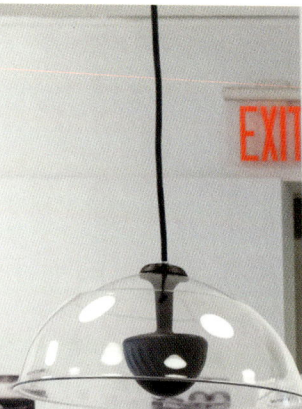

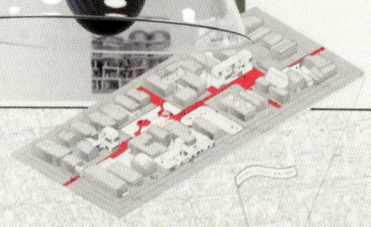

How to Start a Club

Interview between Poppy Levison and Finnegan Shannon

The Anti-Stairs Club Lounge is an artist intervention, protests and participatory artwork. The first iteration of the project was created by Finnegan Shannon in 2017 at the Wassaic Project in New York State. Addressing the inaccessibility of the project's exhibition space, the lounge was created exclusively for visitors who cannot or choose not to go up stairs.

In 2019 Shannon held a new iteration of the Anti-Stairs Club Lounge in response to Thomas Heatherwick's Vessel. The Vessel is a $150 million structure located in Hudson Yard, New York, composed of a honeycomb-like lattice made up of 154 flights of stairs, or 2,500 steps. This iteration of Shannon's Anti-Stairs Club Lounge challenged the inaccessibility, both symbolic and actual, of the Vessel – asking who public space and art is for if it excludes disabled people.

Poppy: Clubs are created either around a common interest – you might go to a sports club or a knitting club – or from a need to find a community. So you might have university societies or clubs or organizations for disabled people or people of colour or other groups that find it harder to find their community. I am curious about how the Anti-Stairs Club was set up as a sort of protest initiative, which isn't normally the foundation for a club. What was the reasoning behind founding a club and how did it go in the initial stage?

Finnegan: When I'm approaching an inaccessible or exclusionary space, I want to connect with other people who feel disillusioned or alienated by that, too. Changing that structure is secondary. Obviously, as one person, it's really hard to make any type of change and I really believe that the most powerful change comes through collective action. And so, for me, the club feels like this. I am ambulatory – I can do some stairs, but I live in New York City which is very inaccessible to me. We have huge problems with our transit system. I live in inaccessible housing and I feel very anti-stairs. I'm always interested in how people identify – or don't – with the term 'Disabled' and in trying to create a more open space of connection. If you also sigh when you meet a staircase, 'Welcome! Come on in!'

Poppy: Broadening notions about accessibility is a theme in your work, but you have also mentioned being silly – it's always really playful, from the cushions with the logo at the Wassaic Project in 2017 to the bright orange beanies distributed at the Anti-Stairs

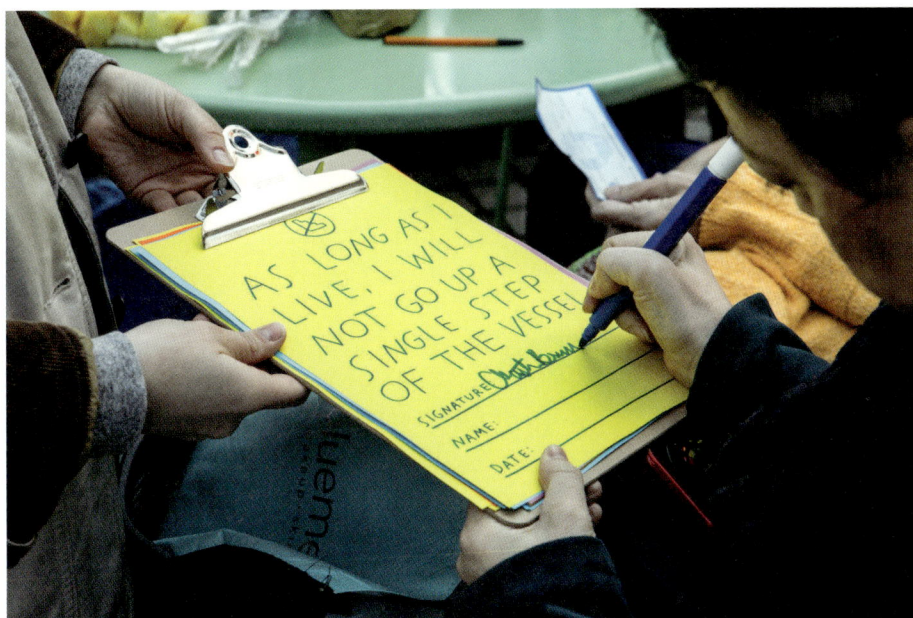

Club Lounge at the Vessel in 2019. The message is partly serious – it clearly means 'anti-stairs' – but it also feels like it's satirizing things. Protest is something that can go either way. It can be very peaceful and all about love, or it can be the complete opposite – really angry and with justified anger about an object like the Vessel, which is entirely stairs. I'm curious about how people respond to that playfulness?

Finnegan: Humour has been a constant thread through my work. I'm sure you've experienced this when you bring up disability or access, especially to non-disabled people – there's this ultra seriousness. People feel very on edge. There's a lot of, 'OK, what's the protocol? What do we do?' And that always feels like such a stark contrast to the way that I live my life as a disabled

person, or the way most of my disabled friends and colleagues live. Humour is such a valuable tool for navigating the relentlessness of hostility towards disability. Sometimes things are just so messed up – at least getting to laugh together about how ridiculous it is can be cathartic.

I'm always trying to include play, togetherness, humour, fun, but also still be very clear. And allowing anger to be part of that. I don't think those are mutually exclusive. And that was definitely the case when I was planning the Anti-Stairs Club Lounge at the Vessel. My goal was really to be angry *together* with other people, and then also to use public space in ways that I'm interested in. What's so upsetting about the Vessel is that it feels like the opposite of what I would want from

public space, and so I was like, 'I wanna just be together and, like, hang out, have snacks, sit down, rest, lounge.' That felt like the most powerful rebuttal of the Vessel. Just to say, 'I'm not interested in that kind of space at all. *This* is what I want from public space.'

Poppy: I think that was made really clear with your posters – where you could sign a statement that read 'As long as I live, I will not go up a single step of the Vessel'. That shows this is not what you would call *your* public space. It's a really nice way of putting it.

I don't know what the rules are in the USA, but having protests is becoming increasingly difficult in the UK, particularly in new developments similar to Hudson Yards. There are areas in London, such as around King's Cross, which have a similar feel and they're actually privately owned public spaces (POPS). I am curious about the logistics, but maybe a good place to start is how easy was it to have a protest in a managed 'public space'?

Finnegan: That was a huge part of the planning process and a real learning curve because I don't come from an urban-design background, so I wasn't familiar with the distinction between, for example, a public park and a POP space and did a lot of research. In New York, Zuccotti Park, where Occupy Wall Street was in 2011, was a POP space and there was a legal ruling that the owner had total agency over what is and isn't allowed in it.

I wanted to do the protest immediately after the Vessel opened. We were trying to scope it out, peering through fences, trying to figure out 'What is this space gonna be like?' I thought we might not be allowed to have signage, so I made this large-format newspaper that had, printed on the inside, an article by scholar and writer Kevin Gotkin on the ableism of the Vessel and, when people were reading it, the outward-facing side of the newspaper just said 'Anti-Stairs Club Lounge'. So, the newspaper acted as publicity for people who wanted to know more about the Vessel and were saying, 'I'm trying to understand, why is this so ableist?' The beanies were also a big part of that. I wanted a strong presence in the space, to be able to distinguish who was 'in the lounge' and who wasn't. But I thought we would probably be asked not to erect any barriers or things like that. The beanies were a way of having this feeling of togetherness, but they couldn't be pointed to as something that wasn't allowed in the space. I also just wanted to be able to pick up and leave really quickly.

We didn't end up having an adversarial relationship with security, but I did appoint a security liaison person and did some safety planning. That was my biggest fear, you know, bringing people into the space and so I wanted just to have some basic safety plans in place.

Poppy: How did you recruit people to come along? What, technically, makes you a club member?

Finnegan: It is definitely like a big tent. You wanna be in the club? You're in the club. You like the club? You're in. Actually, I should roll that back a little bit – you do have to agree not go up a single step of the Vessel. I felt like that was the bare minimum of solidarity required. Obviously for me, or for other disabled friends who are wheelchair users, signing that document was like, 'Yeah, of course!' But for people who have a less negative relationship with stairs, asking for that was a way of being in solidarity – if you want to be part of our thing, you can't be part of *that* thing.

Poppy: How did you get a group there? Did you already have people?

Finnegan: Again, it was a different process because I was probably overcareful, but I was trying to be really secret about it. I really didn't want the developer, Related, to get wind of something happening.

Around that time, like 2017, 2018, 2019, there was a really intentional effort to organize disabled artists in New York City: there was a group called DANT (Disability/Arts/NYC Task Force) that was doing some local lobbying; and the disabled dancer Alice Shepherd and Kinetic Light – the Disability Arts Assembly – were hosting informal gatherings. I always like to say that so much of what has been possible for me comes from this really intentional effort to connect people, because it is really hard. Disability can be really isolating and I am a beneficiary of that moment, of trying to know each other more, locally. So, for the action at the Vessel, I had some people who I had connected with, through work and disability arts and community, who I was able to email. I did a post on social media that was kind of vague: 'We're doing an Anti-Stairs Club Lounge thing. Let me know if you wanna join,' but not saying specifically where.

And I did also invite non-disabled friends, though it was important for me to only invite people who didn't need me to explain why I was upset. I really wanted the group to feel like people were participating because they wanted to, and because they were angry too, and not try so hard to convince people.

Poppy: You mentioned a slight fear about not wanting to disclose what was happening. I'm curious about whether you ever got a specific response from either Heatherwick Studios or the developers of the area?

Finnegan: Not even one iota of acknowledgement, I think. The Vessel, in that period right after it opened, it was so popular I thought maybe even just geotagging on Instagram would at least make us show up as a little blip. But so many people were posting so many photos of that location at that time. There was nothing – I've never heard from Heatherwick Studios; I've never heard from Related. I was in touch with Elizabeth F. Emens, a lawyer who was doing research. There actually was a legal challenge about the inaccessibility

of the Vessel later on and she did a lot of research trying to trace if any of that came back to the Anti-Stairs Club Lounge, but couldn't find any evidence of that.

Poppy: What has been the response to the Vessel from disabled people?

Finnegan: So many people I know were just like, 'What? What is this like? And why?' We're so often told things can't be accessible because it's historic architecture, because of existing building structures and because of budget, and so to have a structure open in 2019 in a brand-new development with a $150 million production budget, it felt like such a slap in the face. And another thing that was on my mind at the time was the artist Park McArthur, who had a show at MoMA earlier that year, maybe late 2018, and part of that project was this imagining of a live workspace for disabled artists.

This piece was part of the audio description for the show, but it was an imagined space drawn from many real-life and imagined spaces. So I think that, also on my mind, was the question 'What could we have had instead?' It was very tongue in cheek, but the official request of the protest was a permanent Anti-Stairs Club Lounge with a $150 million production budget.

Poppy: It feels like architecture currently doesn't value the experience of disabled people, just slaps you in the face with how much they don't value disabled

experience – over $100 million dollars worth of not caring. And that is quite shocking.

Finnegan: I will say one thing – and you might have noticed already – but there is actually an elevator in the Vessel. I believe it was added later due to pressure from a disabled advisory committee, but to me that's always felt totally irrelevant, in terms of ethos of the design. The framing of the Vessel is all about 'the climb'. I think people get confused. I mean, it's such a powerful diversion tool to be able to say, 'Oh yeah, there's an elevator.' But it's not a building where you would take an elevator up and then you could move around on the floor, because it's literally up and down stairs on every level – there are 80 platforms and I believe the elevator was running to two of them. When you look at what kind of accessibility that's offering, it's miniscule.

Poppy: Jos Boys, the co-director of DisOrdinary Architecture – a disabled-led platform that works with disabled artists and designers to explore new ways to think about disability in architecture and design, in both discourse and practice – has this great way of describing how architects treat disabled people like little cells that need to be moved around. No one thinks about their experience: the whole point of the Vessel is the experience of climbing up something. It's about gaining height at a certain pace, using stairs within a structure to get different views. If it was just about getting to a height, it would be a platform with lifts and stairs that were all encased in something like a tower. But the whole premise of the design is moving up and through it. That freedom doesn't exist with a lift, even if on paper it's, 'Well, a disabled person can get from the bottom to the top, yeah.'

But to pivot away from the Vessel – since then you've worked with institutions, putting in Anti-Stairs Club Lounges. How has it been, working *with* organizations as opposed to protesting against someone?

Finnegan: The first iteration – before the Vessel version – was at an arts organization called the Wassaic Project, which supports emerging artists. They do these really big, vibrant group exhibitions, with sometimes 50 to 70 emerging artists. The exhibition space used to be a mill building. It's basically a repurposed agricultural building, an extremely vertical space, with seven storeys and no elevator. As a disabled artist and someone who really wants to centre other disabled people as the primary audience for my work, is there a way for me to engage with those types of spaces? The first iteration of the project was literally a lounge – it was an enclosed room on the ground floor that had chairs and reading materials, and chilled seltzer and my favourite candy and a charging station (p.83).

But, similar to our protest at the Vessel, it was a space exclusively for people who are *not* going up stairs. There was actually a key code on the door, and to get the key code you had to sign a little thing at the front desk saying, 'I'm not going upstairs.' That was, in some ways, a very practical thing: I'm in a lot of situations where I'm with a group and some people want to walk farther or go somewhere else that I don't have the energy or capacity for, so I often find myself waiting around. It seemed supportive to have a nice place to wait, to acknowledge that something has been added to the experience rather than just about missing out.

Poppy: So often there's this feeling with disabled spaces of wanting to include *everyone*, but you're excluding people who already have access to other things, which I think is really interesting. Which leads on really well to one of the most common comments that I get, to the point that we kind of have an architecture-school disability conversation bingo: 'How do you balance diverse access needs?'

Even in architecture school, if someone proposes a project about disability, tutors are very quick to say that the definition of disability is too broad. You need to specify: design a school for the blind or design a building for autistic people. But, from my own experience, when you get a group of disabled people together in a room, we're actually pretty good at understanding and meeting each other's access needs. What are your experiences of having really diverse groups of disabled

85

people? Should you focus on something that's inaccessible rather than focusing on a disability?

Finnegan: Wow, so much there! I guess, for lack of a better term, the main tenet of my practice is 'cross-disability solidarity'. That's definitely something I've learned from other disabled artists and from performance group Sins Invalid's 10 Principles of Disability Justice. It's something I really think about all the time. There's so much we don't know about other people's access needs.

It's always an iterative process and there's lots that I look back on, from years ago, and think, 'Oof, yeah, I missed the mark on that.' People get really caught up in an abstract theoretical place, but there is a difference between building a building that's going to be around for hundreds of years and a temporary installation. The process is iterative and I'm open to feedback. If I'm in touch and in tune with the people who are involved, I find it much easier to try things and experiment.

The other thing that often comes up is that we don't all need to have identical access. I think about it sometimes as a menu of different entry points – as long as different modes of experience are being given attention and are being valued, they don't necessarily have to be totally one to one. Inaccessibility feels really bad: when you're taking the accessible route and you're in the back of halls, you're passing boxes and you

feel, 'OK, nobody actually gave this any real kind of care.' I don't mind going a different route, but I want that route to have been respected.

Poppy: Yes, it should be treated in the same way as the rest of the building. It should be as beautifully finished as any other space. One of the reasons we end up with a really crappy experience for disabled people is that there are hardly any disabled people in architecture – there are loads of barriers to entering architecture, but particularly accessibility. I think the conversation in architecture is a lot further behind than the disability arts movement, which in the UK (and I think in the USA as well) is thriving. You've mentioned having a bigger community, so I wonder what you think architecture, but also other disciplines, could take from what you have learned through the disability arts movement.

Finnegan: The feeling that I often get from architects is that compliance, which has been central to thinking about access and disability, has set up this really antagonistic relationship. And that's obviously also because disabled people have not been part of those conversations, but one of the things that I really value about working within an arts context is that it's not solution oriented, necessarily. We don't have to figure it out within the project – we can point to something or ask a question or be curious about something.

In the realm of architecture, because

projects are so massive, so expensive, and there are so many stakeholders, I imagine it can be harder to have a 'let's throw it at the wall and see if it sticks' approach. But I do feel this – especially from disabled architects – is that disability is a generative force. It's a creative part of any type of making, and I certainly feel that in my art practice: thinking about accessibility is what enriches and guides my practice. There are obviously lots of reasons why that attitude is hard to access under capitalism, and other strictures of oppression that we exist within, but when I can, it's such a pleasure to dream and fantasize.

Poppy: I was thinking of the themes that run through your work, and particularly about the benches you place in exhibitions that invite people to sit down if they agree with a statement (often about rest and fatigue) displayed on the bench. They're so legible and comprehensible that it's easy to understand the message you're trying to get across. And they're really good at involving non-disabled people or people who wouldn't necessarily think of themselves as someone with access needs – older people or people who just can't stand up for too long, or whatever it might be. It gets those people on board with what you're trying to say really quickly. And so, in that context, you talked earlier about having a big tent, but I'm interested to know how important you think allies are? How much focus do you think should be put on getting people on board?

Finnegan: That's a great question. I think most systems of domination – like ableism – aren't working well for anyone. Even people who consider themselves non-disabled are struggling with the demands that ableist, racist, classist structures are putting on their lives. Understanding that the way things are is not neutral or immutable is part of the gift that disability brings. My hope with that work is that people have an embodied experience that something could be different, and maybe not even related to what they need themselves.

Maybe they don't need seating, but this might open the door for people to question the structure. I've made a really intentional choice in my practice to centre disabled people. That is where I want to put my time and energy, and that's where I feel I can make the most exciting work, and I actually think it's a really effective way to get non-disabled people on board. When people see how cool and fun some of the things that we're doing are there is a power shift where they think, 'Ooh, I am interested in that' or 'I do want to be part of that', which I think is really different than the way disability has historically, and continually, been pushed away.

So that's been my approach. I'm going to do the thing that I want to do, with my friends and community and network, and if you want to be a part of this, if this is a draw to you, then, yeah, come on in.

Poppy: Nice. And then a final question. Which of the Anti-Stairs Club Lounge

87

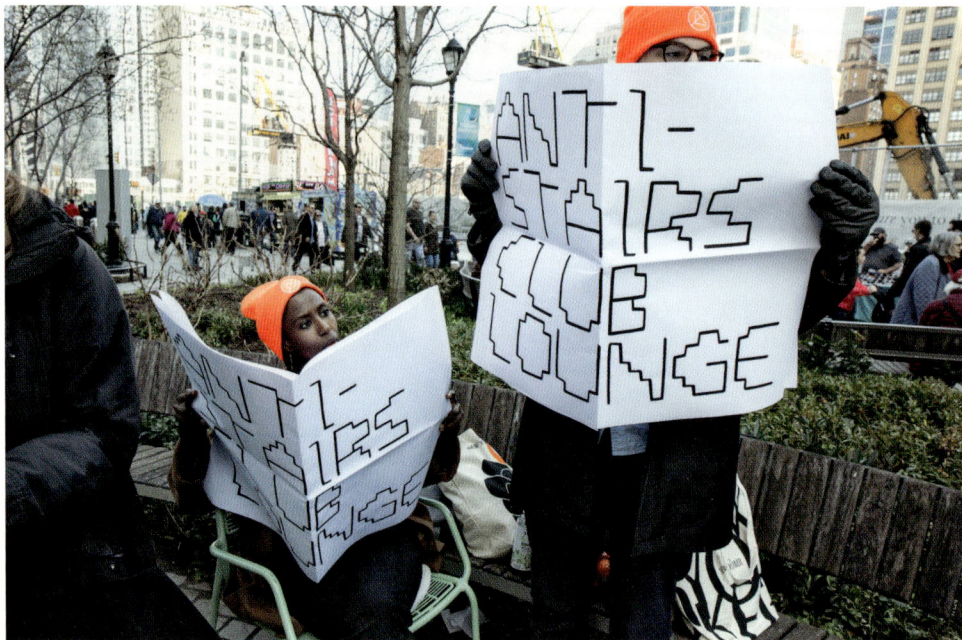

88

iterations has been your favourite? Or what element do you think has been the most impactful?

Finnegan: I think one of my favourite things, that I didn't really plan but which has been such an ongoing delight, is the fact that the beanies from Anti-Stairs Club Lounge have been dispersed. Everyone was welcome to take their beanie and then other people have requested one. I've sent them to different people and I just love the way that the protest then gets distributed into all these other spaces. I think about it often when I'm wearing my Anti-Stairs Club Lounge hat in the subway system in New York – I am my own little Anti-Stairs Club Lounge. And I am grumpy and upset about the inaccessibility and what's happening here.

Every once in a while I hear from friends or people who say, 'I saw someone in this place and they were wearing that hat and so we got to talk about it.' That's been really exciting to me and I've continued to make the hats because I want them to go out into the world as much as possible.

Above: Poppy Levison in the Anti-Stairs Club Lounge beanie that her mother requested for her from Finnegan Shannon after The Vessel event (see opposite)

How to Protest

**Essay by Natalie Kane, with illustrations
by Seo Hye Lee and Access Power Visibility**

How should we work collectively to achieve our desired
political futures as disabled people? Can technology
create opportunities for new relationships and
behaviours, and when does it complicate matters? With
the Proxy Protest Tool, a project created and iterated
upon by Arjun Harrison-Mann, Benjamin Redgrove
and Kaiya Waerea and a community of collaborators,
everyday objects are repurposed to make political
protest accessible to everyone, wherever they might be.

Harrison-Mann and Redgrove met at the Royal College of Art, London, in 2015 and quickly found common ground, mainly in following a shared Do It With Others (DIWO) ethos that places collaboration at the centre of their design practices. DIWO is a method of co-creation that springs from new-media art culture, including the arts organization Furtherfield which established the practice of moving away from 'top-down initiations into co-produced, networked artistic activities'.[1]

In their final year of studying, they found collaborators in disability justice activist group Disabled People Against Cuts (DPAC) working together to ask questions about how technology could be used to reach communities that are excluded from traditional methods of protest, and what systemic barriers they might face.

Protesting in public is not always an option for disabled communities. Many people cannot leave their houses or

91

make difficult journeys into city centres for a multitude of reasons, such as lack of public toilets, arranging care, or the inaccessibility of public transport and the prohibitive cost of bridging this gap. There's also the matter of the protest itself – there are particular risks for disabled people at protests as routes are not often planned with accessibility in mind, and there is the potential for kettling by the police which can deny access to medication and scheduled care. Much protest and action by disabled people has, of necessity, moved online.

Proxy Protest was set up in the context of years of cuts to disability benefits: in 2010 major austerity cuts by David Cameron's Conservative government affected disabled people disproportionately, with research by the University of York, released in 2021, linking the impact of cuts in social and healthcare to 57,550 more deaths than would have been expected between 2010 and 2014.[2] Between 2012 and 2019, 335,000 additional deaths were attributed by the Glasgow Centre for Population Health to spending cuts to public services and benefits which disproportionately affected disabled and marginalized communities.[3] In an attempt to span digital and physical space, Harrison-Mann, Redgrove and their collaborators created the first Power Tool, named as such to empower all participants in protest. It was an online livestream tool that paired onsite with offsite participants – with British Sign Language (BSL), audio description and live subtitling all provided by other members on the site. It was enabled by a harness-worn mobile phone worn by a 'proxy', which was accessed through a laptop by the remote user, wherever they might be.

For the first trial of the Power Tool, in April 2019, Benjamin Redgrove 'proxied' for a member of DPAC at Facebook Headquarters to protest discriminatory treatment of disability-related pages including examples where content made by disabled people had been flagged as 'disturbing' by Facebook's moderation tools. Several members of the protest wore the first version of the harness, fitted with a mobile phone loaded with an early version of the tool. This first trial gave the wearer a sense of what

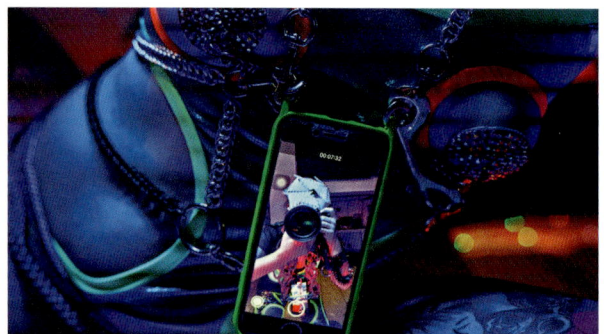

it meant to be a proxy and tested the experience both for the proxy and the remote user.

The next iteration of the Power Tool was implemented as part of the 2019 Serpentine Power Walks, a series of guided neighbourhood walks under the aegis of the Serpentine Gallery, London, each highlighting a different aspect of the city: the histories of resistance, issues with social housing, low-wage work and accessibility. DPAC's tour through the London borough of Westminster, where UK central government is situated, included four disabled participants online, enabled by proxies. It was designed to bring attention to the disproportionate and adverse effects of welfare cuts on disabled people since 2010, and told stories of an earlier protest involving underwear strung up outside the Department of Work and Pensions to mock the then Secretary of State Iain Duncan Smith for an expenses claim he had made for his own underwear.

Designer and publisher Kaiya Waerea was acting as a proxy for the Serpentine walks. In an interview they spoke about the experience of being a proxy for a member of DPAC:

> It was very moving for me to take on that direct responsibility of another, being a sort of surrogate for them in those physical places for others to interact with. Because they were visibly present on the screen, it wasn't just between me and him, other people were approaching me and talking to him through my body.[4]

Becoming a proxy is an expression of access intimacy, a complex concept defined by writer, educator and community organizer Mia Mingus (see p. 64) as 'that elusive, hard to describe feeling when someone else "gets" your access needs ... It could also be the way your body relaxes and opens up with someone when all your access needs are being met.'[5] It does not need to be expressly or explicitly political, but something that enables a disabled person to participate with fewer barriers, whatever they might be. When acting as proxy, those who are not in attendance are trusting that you will hold their values and identity safe – an unusual but important role.

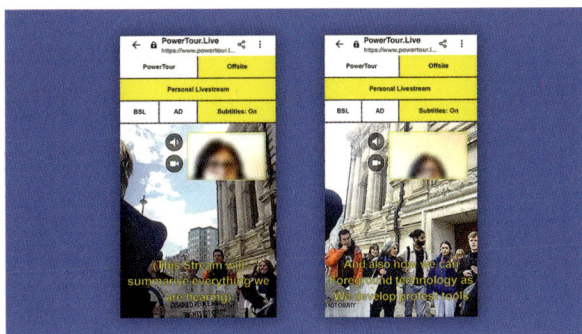

93

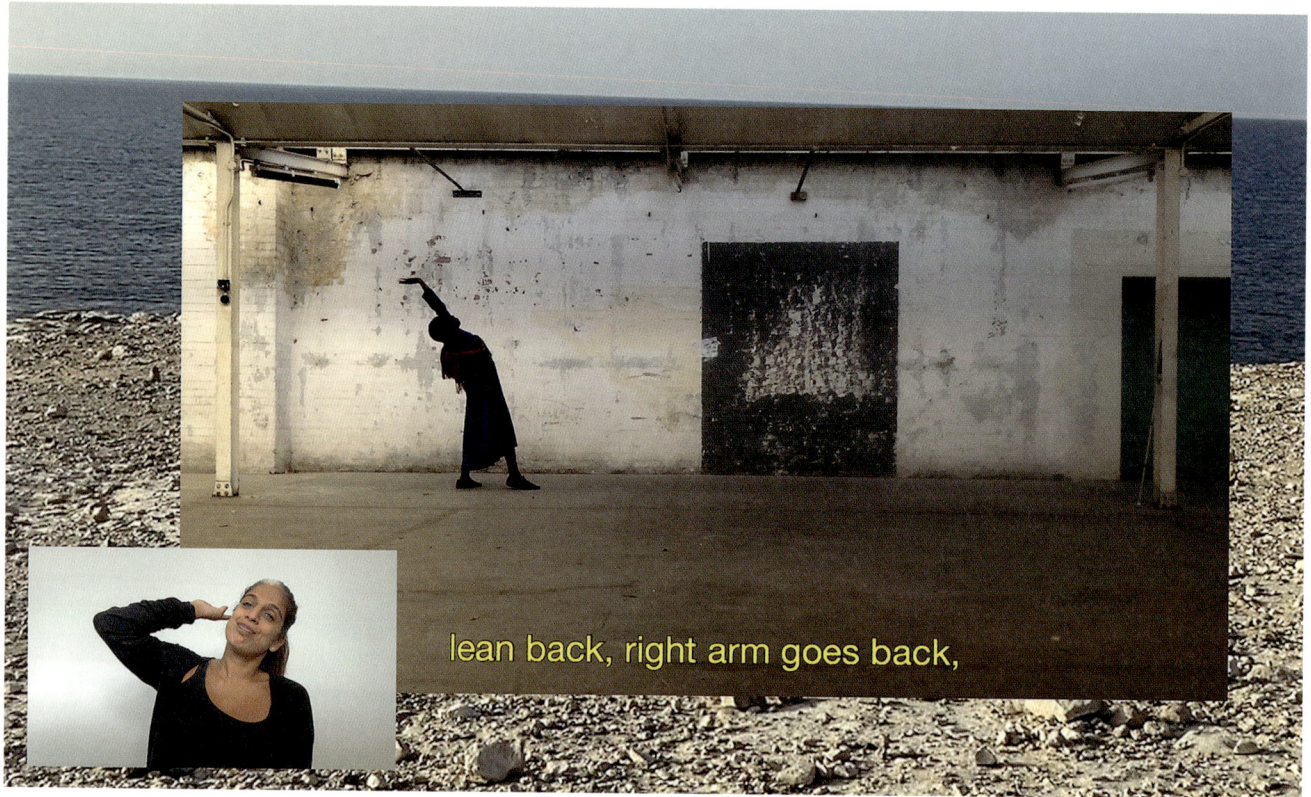

lean back, right arm goes back,

In 2019 Waerea joined Harrison-Mann and Redgrove to form Access Power Visibility (APV), a collective built around disability justice and 'radical accessibility', using the Social Model of Disability as a design provocation.[6] In early 2020 the whole project was renamed Proxy Power Tool to highlight the role of the proxy in access and to reflect better the closely held relationship between the wearer and viewer. APV engaged with artists and designers to create the film exhibit *Perspectives on Visibility* in 2020 when Covid-19 was particularly affecting disabled communities. There were three films exploring access across distance using the Proxy Power Tool. Artist and designer Sky Cubacub (see pp 108, 116–19)

collaborated with photographer Sandra Oviedo, aka Colectivo Multipolar, for the film *Hot Pink Chain*, centring around Sky's garment-making practice that aims to make queer disability 'radically visible'.[7] In *Outside Inside* (above), Ebony Rose Dark, a visually impaired Black drag performance artist, asked what it means to be seen, by mapping space and the natural world through live audio-described choreography. Sophie Hoyle's film *Hyper Vigilantes* tackled the sickbed, drawing a line between public and private spheres by broadcasting the words of sick writers and artists.

The tool started to evolve as the landscape of protest rapidly changed with shifting Covid legislation, major

protest movements, such as those mobilizing around the murder of George Floyd in 2020, and the increased momentum of Black Lives Matter. Questioning what accessibility to protest meant in lockdown, particularly for at-risk communities that wanted to participate, APV developed an online DIY guide to Proxy Protest. A process of 'undesigning' the tool occurred, as the team realized that their initial design was potentially too prescriptive, with the existing harness being the only way in which a tool could be worn – potentially limiting potential wearers. It also looked like a body-worn camera which was too reminiscent of police surveillance equipment, although initially this was a deliberate attempt by the designers to subvert surveillance aesthetics.

APV ran multiple workshops with activists, disabled people, academics, design students and other collaborators to test both the tool itself and how the harness could best answer many different access needs. The custom harness, previously a black strap and laser-cut black mobile-phone holder, became something altogether more accessible – the slicker version replaced by an entirely DIY one. For Liberty Festival, an event celebrating Deaf, Disabled and neurodivergent artists as part of Lewisham London Borough of Culture 2022, the DIY guide was further developed into the free Proxy Protest Tool Kit. This 'lo-fi' kit contained a scarf, rubber bands and a two-colour Risograph-printed instruction booklet (chosen for its low production cost) on putting the tool together. APV released the step-by-step online, enabling anyone, anywhere, to create their own wearable proxy harness.

The Proxy Protest Power Tool has moved through several digital guises as well as physical, evolving to subvert existing platforms originally used for messaging and social networking. Having originally been a custom-built platform, APV found that a custom platform required significant maintenance by the team. Handing control to users to create a kit of tools that suited them allowed for decentralization of the project. Users can now use anything they like to set up a proxy, provided they consider the security of their connection. APV provide a list of suggested apps, such as Signal, for making calls, and suggest privacy-first

behaviours including an avatar if the user isn't comfortable sharing their face on screen. Other tools, such as face-blurring filters, are also part of the suite of tools suggested for collaborating with a proxy.

The project has become inherently less technological and more rooted in behaviours and community dynamics, encouraging protest movements to consider the access requirements of others, ensuring that the BSL interpreter is in sight and ensuring you move away from noise that may be difficult for those with sensory sensitivities. Proxies are encouraged to maintain good protest etiquette because of the unique position they have in wearing a recording device. They must ensure that attendees' faces are out of sight, which is particularly important to protect already marginalized communities.

APV have created a community dynamic built on mutual trust and care, enabled by a set of DIY tools that can be adapted to multiple needs and requirements. Participants can 'show up' for their communities in ways previously unattainable to them, and be present in a blurring of digital and physical space. Rooted in disability-first perspectives, both from the designers and their collaborators, the Proxy Protest Power Tool enables access to political life, imagining new possibilities for protest.

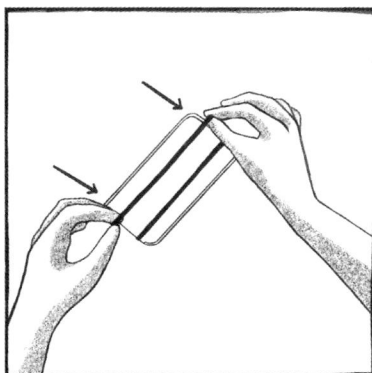

1. Stretch two elastic bands over the length of the empty smartphone case, at regular intervals and avoid obscuring the camera.

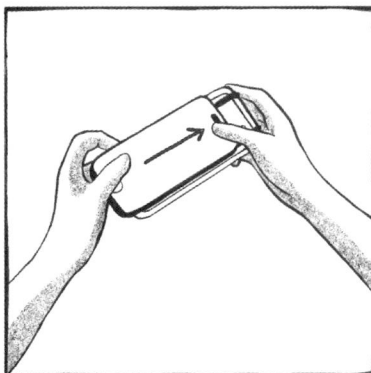

2. Put the smartphone in the case, making sure the two elastic bands are still in position.

3. The elastic bands should now be comfortably sandwiched between the smartphone and case, which should also still be securely together. If the smartphone and case do not still fit together, they won't stay secure and should not be used.

4. Turning the phone over, check the elastic bands run vertically down the back of the phone case.

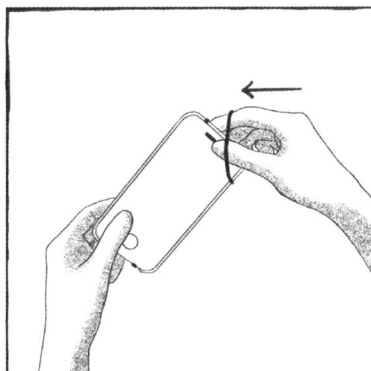

5. Loop the third elastic band over the top of the smartphone.

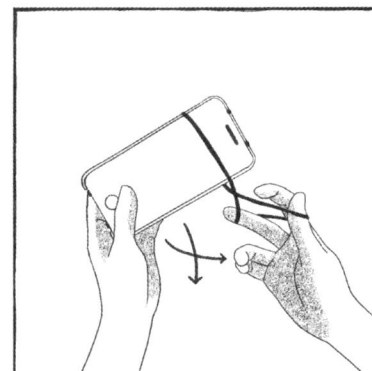

6. Once looped over, pull and twist the elastic band so that it crosses over itself at its centre.

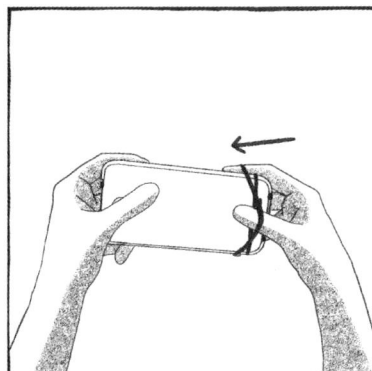

7. Pull the elastic band back over the top of the smartphone again. The two loops should now tightly and securely sit across the width of the phone. If they do not feel secure, you may need to use an elastic band with a smaller diameter.

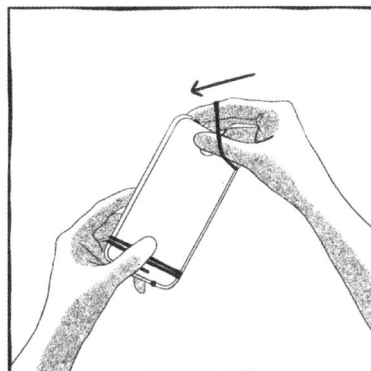

8. Repeat this process with the fourth elastic band, at the bottom of the phone.

9. As before, once looped over pull and twist the elastic band so that it crosses over itself in the centre.

97

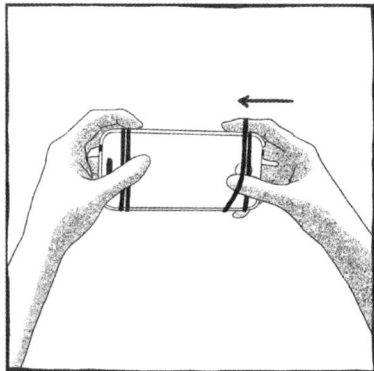

10. Pull the elastic band back over the top of the smartphone again. The two loops should now tightly and securely sit across the width of the phone. If they do not feel secure, you may need to use an elastic band with a smaller diameter.

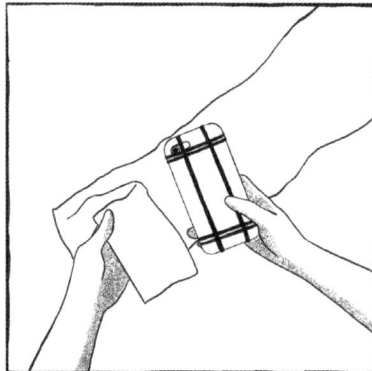

11. Check your sash material will fit underneath the two vertically stretched elastic bands. The two bands should be loose enough to allow the sash underneath, but tight enough to keep the sash in place if the elastic bands aren't lifted.

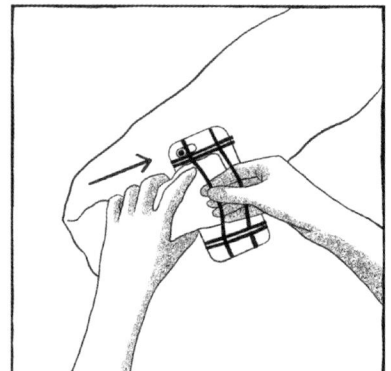

12. Feed the sash underneath these two elastic bands.

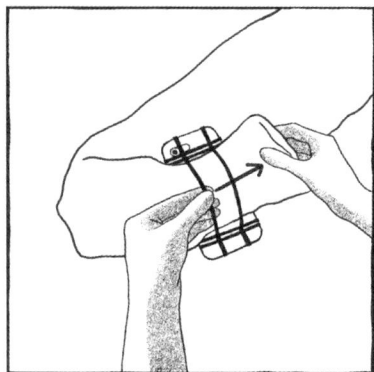

13. Keep feeding the sash through until the smartphone is roughly in the middle of the material.

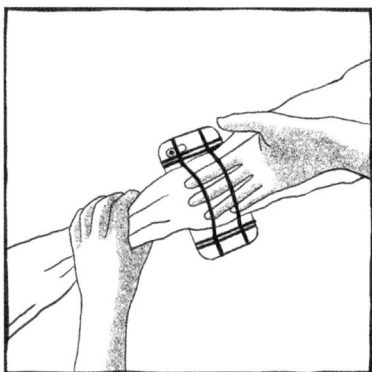

14. You may need to make adjustments to ensure the sash doesn't catch against the elastic.

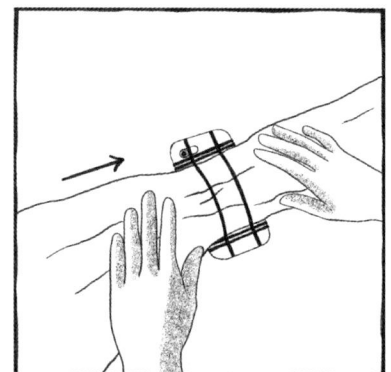

15. Once happy with the position, flatten and smooth the sash out.

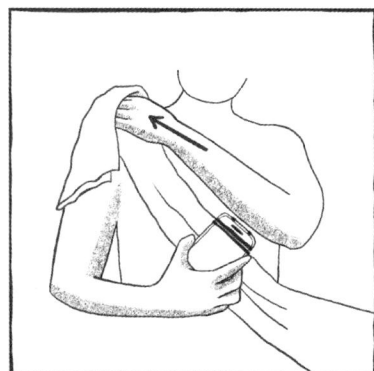

16. Holding the smartphone in one hand position the sash diagonally across your torso.

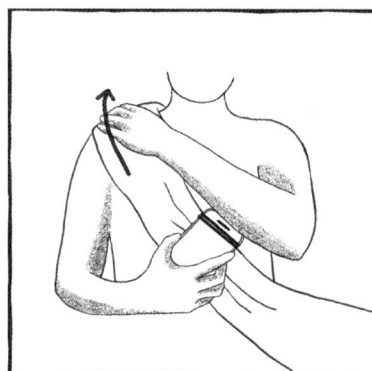

17. Take one end of the sash over your shoulder.

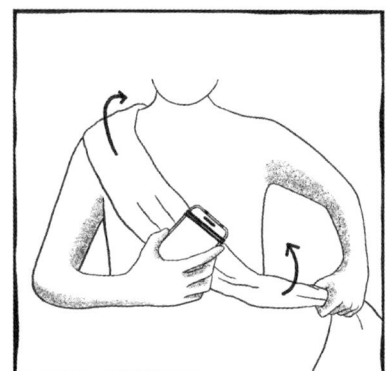

18. Take the other end of the sash around the lower torso and check you are happy with how the sash and smartphone sit.

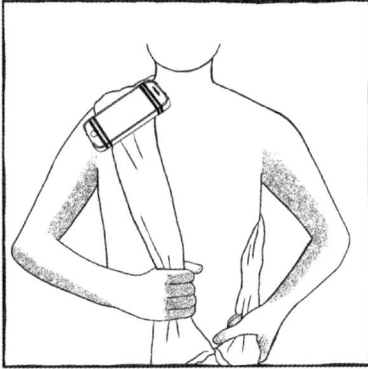

19. Bring the ends of the sash to the front in order to tie them together.

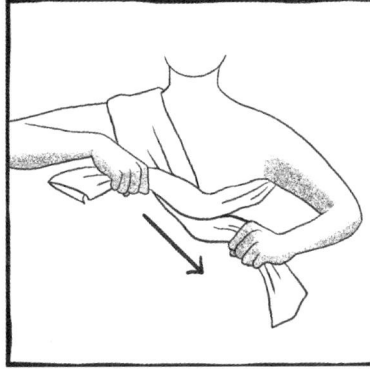

20. You may want to use some form of fastener or double knot.

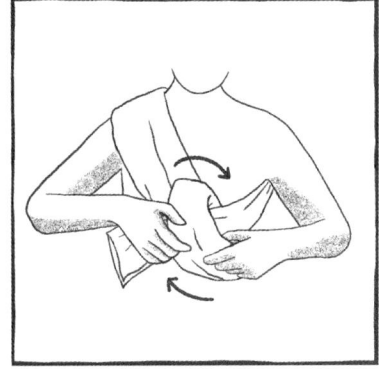

21. Use a knotting method you feel works with the material, is secure and comfortable.

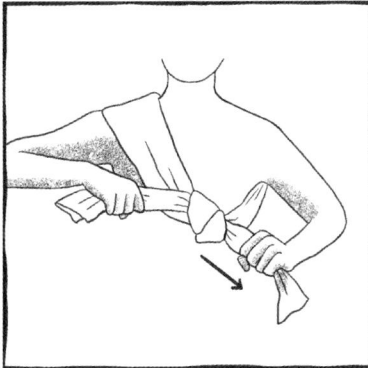

22. Pull the camera around to the front again.

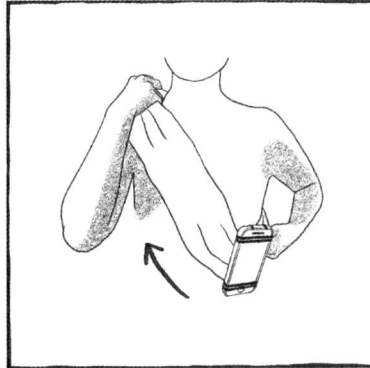

23. Attach headphones and any other accessories you may want to use to communicate with your offsite counterpart.

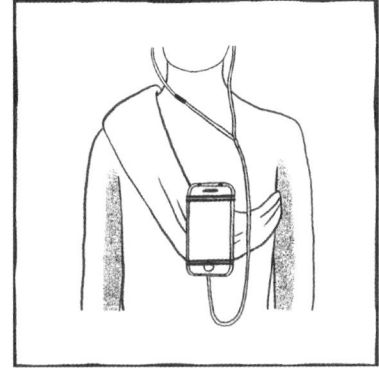

24. Take the other end of the sash around the lower torso and check you are happy with how the sash and smartphone sit.

How to Make an Image

**Interview between Reuben Liebeskind
and Jameisha Prescod**

Jameisha Prescod and Reuben Liebeskind discuss image making, sickness, pain and race, traversing the range of media that Prescod employs. From filmmaking, to photography and social media, this interview explores crip approaches to image production and how visual media can be used to process, connect and educate about sickness and disability.

You Look Okay to Me, the online platform founded and directed by Prescod, explores the social and cultural aspects of living with a chronic condition through visual media. Since the project's inception, the community has grown to over 40,000 online across all social platforms. Much of the work on You Look Okay to Me explores issues of health injustice, examining the intersections at which people experience medical inequality, such as race, class and gender.

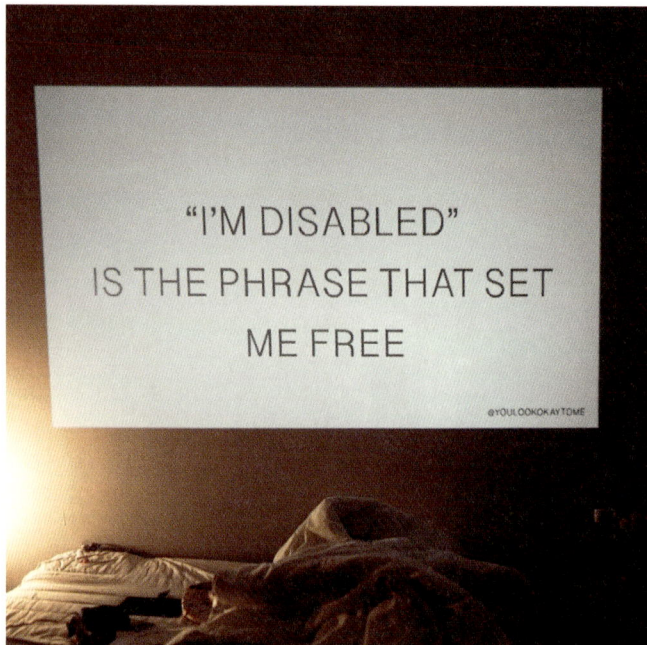

"I'M DISABLED"
IS THE PHRASE THAT SET
ME FREE

@YOULOOKOKAYTOME

Reuben: You describe your Instagram page, You Look Okay to Me, as a digital space for chronically ill people. Could you tell us how it began and how it has changed into what it is today?

Jameisha: You Look Okay to Me started, technically, at university in around 2016. I started my course and got diagnosed with lupus at exactly the same time. I was on a film course, so I was really struggling to fit in and do the same things my peers were. So I wanted to create a small project that interviewed a couple of people with chronic illnesses to explore that, and then there was a little competition – I had to come up with a name and I was like, 'Oh, yeah, sure – You Look Okay To Me, is fine.' But it didn't just end as the small series I was planning. It grew into this Instagram page where I would just do little posts and then it grew into video essays. Over the years it's transformed into a space that explores illness and disability in general, whereas originally it was just a project that allowed me to talk about illness but also explore my skills in film without the pressure of being on set for 16 hours a day – doing it my own way. But it has changed a lot since then.

Reuben: Sick people, often of necessity, find ways to bend, subvert or repurpose design. Could you speak a bit about how you do this with social media?

Jameisha: I speak about Instagram specifically because that's the main one I'm on. At face value, social media's purpose often is to show out, to benefit people that are fashionable and post outfits and content like that. It often doesn't really seem like a space where you can talk about disability, because it feels like a topic that's not pushed. Ultimately I found I had to redesign how I wanted to speak to people and how to use the tools, and exploit the advantages or the little loopholes I could get from Instagram to start conversations and build community. Even right now I post knitting content, but it's actually chronic illness content because I know knitting content does well. But I'm always having to 'Trojan horse' chronic illness into conversations in a sense, which allows us to have conversations that push boundaries, speak truth to power. I've also had people who get help because of the question feature we use on Instagram: there is one person, who has migraines, and has no one, and they were like, 'I

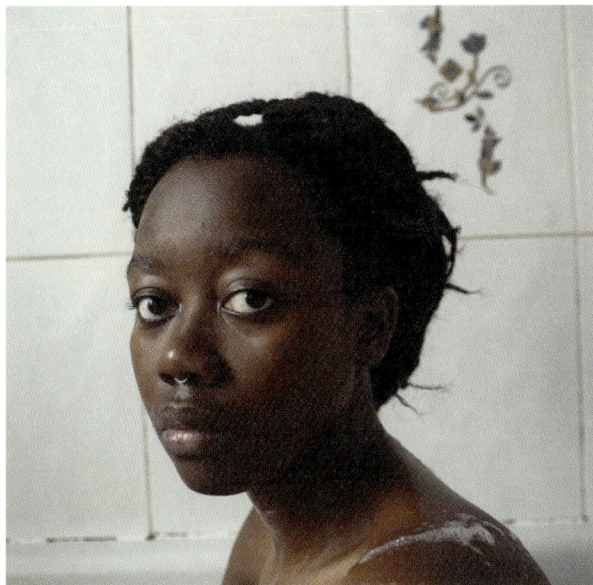

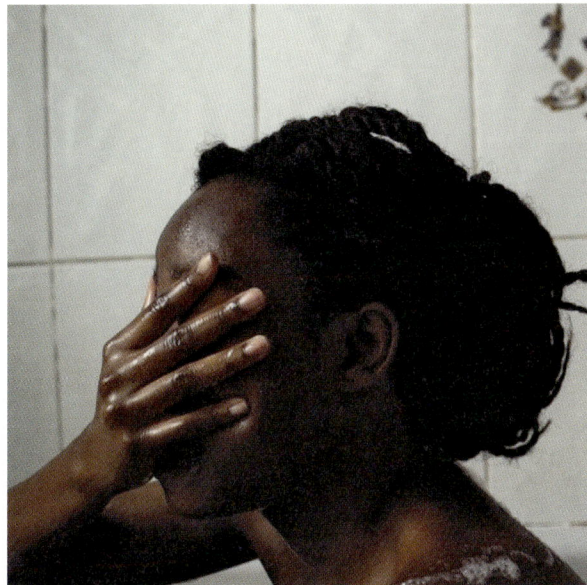

really can't find anyone.' So I asked my community, and all these responses come back: 'Speak to this person.' The tools are not necessarily designed for that, and yet we're able to use them to improve our lives, and also connect with each other across country lines.

Reuben: I was wondering if you could talk a little bit more about disabled community building on social media and the relationship that has to You Look Okay to Me.

Jameisha: When I started I didn't have community in mind. Originally, I was just doing a page. But then I realized that the key thing that helps build community over a platform like You Look Okay to Me is the idea of saying, 'Me too!' (not in the context, obviously, of how it's been used recently, but in the context of illness). For example, something happens

to me in hospital and I've just posted about it, put my face on it, was raw, and someone else says 'I had that same experience.' That's usually where the community building starts – from people feeling similarities and feeling seen, and not feeling like they're the only person that's gone through something, which is why I started You Look Okay to Me in the first place.

It's accessible in the sense that, before social media, I wouldn't have had the opportunity to be in a community with someone who has a chronic illness in Indonesia or the United Arab Emirates or in the USA. We're able to have conversations and see the similarities and differences in our experiences. This is more apparent because of Covid. A lot of our organizing and some of the political work has been done from bed, on the phone – some friendships and connections have been built simply in that way. It reimagines what community can look like because, originally, it felt like community was something that could only be built in person, or on the ground, when actually now – not just with my platform but with others – that's not always the case. In fact it's *often* not the case for us.

Reuben: Thinking specifically about algorithmic hostility towards topics concerning disability on the main social media platforms, which seem primarily places for people to show off particular types of lifestyles, I'd like to ask you what you think it means to have You Look Okay to Me on a platform that is, by design, hostile to those who are trying to reach and represent Black and disabled users and creators?

Jameisha: I think to hold space for underrepresented people gives me a bit of purpose. I do like doing it. It makes me feel like I should be continuing. But there is a frustration because these platforms are not designed with disabled people in mind. They are particularly also not designed for Black, disabled, queer, any kind of thing that gets added to that. It's harder. It can be frustrating because it feels like I constantly have to get the message out, and, for it to be seen and to support a whole space, I have to be really flexible and fluid. I have to move with the times and, if something is not working, I have to figure it out, and say, 'Okay cool, we're gonna have to move.' That's with everyone on socials, but it feels particularly apparent for people like me.

It can be fun in the sense that I have to come up with new concepts and new ways of doing things. But it's like, 'Why can't I just talk about it? And it be seen?' That is a bit frustrating. But I have to ask myself often, 'Well, what would you rather be doing?' And so that's the part that keeps me going.

Reuben: There is, of course, a long and radical tradition of self-portraiture being used for self- and communal advocacy, from Frida Kahlo and Claude Cahun to Jo Spence, Maude Salter and Donald Rodney. Throughout the iterations of You Look Okay to Me, you have used images of yourself and shared your personal experiences. I was wondering if you could speak about the importance of the relationship between self-portraiture and advocacy in your work.

Jameisha: Even sharing my own face on social media was a large challenge. And it's weird because most of my work now is very self-reflective. But, actually, I'm very shy and it's very confronting. But at first, with You Look Okay to Me, my face wasn't in it and no one followed the page. And then someone said to me 'How can you expect vulnerability from people talking about a disability if you're not offering up yourself to them and you're not having an exchange?' So, from then on, I got more comfortable doing that. I realized, as well, that for me to both communicate and reflect ideas of disability, I needed to look at myself because I think there were things that were unresolved.

I think about people like Carolee Schneemann, the artist whose work was really centred on the concept of the person and the body in politics. To have that sense of reflection and to put myself on there really allowed me to deepen my disabled politics and put it out there. If I think about the photo *Untangling* (p.107), it's reflecting a concept of disability that we hide a lot. It's about hiding so much but forcing myself not to hide. It's almost like it pushed my politics and my art forward because I'm having to force myself to have all of me present as a disabled person, rather than hide from the expectations of what we're expected to do for capitalism, if that makes sense.

Reuben: You're touching on something really important, which is that as chronically ill people – and this is prevalent in lots of different disabled people's experiences – when we're feeling particularly awful the urge is to think 'I'm just going to stay at home.' And so much of what we go through becomes invisible, often through what I might call 'coercive choices'. For example, at one level I'm choosing to stay in. But on another level, if I lived in an environment that was accepting of me when I was at my sickest, I would probably feel much more comfortable going outside or participating in public life at every point in my experiences of illness. I think that there's something important about bringing your whole self to your work and being able to integrate it through your image-based working.

Jameisha: Yeah. I think if it weren't for a lot of us disabled people doing self-portraiture, you wouldn't see us in art because people haven't willingly, especially historically, represented disabled people in art in a way that felt layered. It was either to ridicule or only portrayed visibly disabled people. It was a spectacle, the few instances in which they were represented in art. Whereas now some of us who've become artists are actually reflecting ourselves. We couldn't count on non-disabled people to do that for us in a way that was also nuanced.

Reuben: Being able to do it on your own terms is important for changing that wider relationship between disabled people and photography, and to image making, because there's historic distrust. Disabled self-portraiture is … I don't think healing is the right word, because I don't know if it's possible to heal such deeply violent legacies, but it's something akin to that.

Living with a chronic illness is isolating and we can often be made to feel invisible, unseen or misunderstood. Much of your work is deeply intimate, occurring within your home. Could you speak about how your work on You Look Okay to Me engages with making visible what's often unseen or unacknowledged and why this is so important to you?

Jameisha: I didn't realize until I started how many conversations, stories or histories were not being spoken about, and were not just ignored but

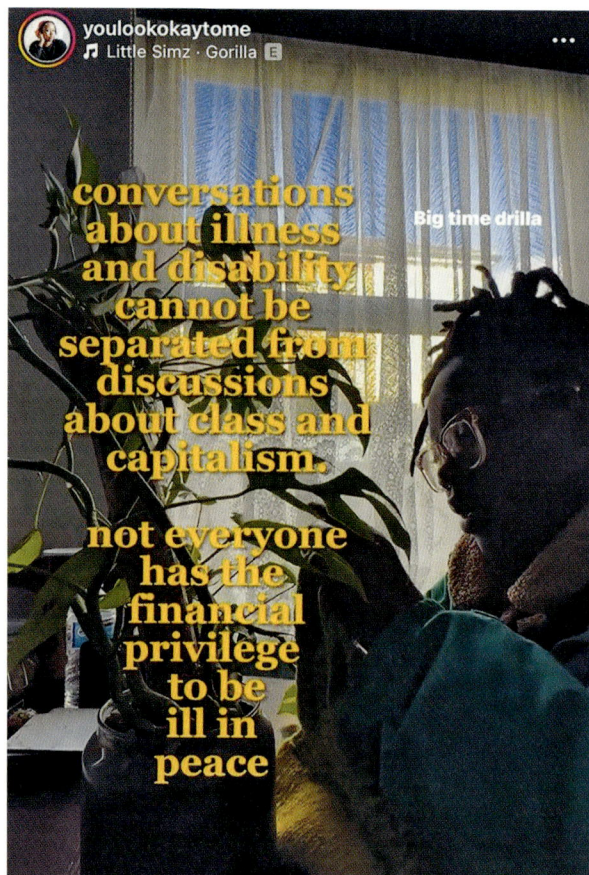

youlookokaytome
♫ Little Simz · Gorilla   E

conversations about illness and disability cannot be separated from discussions about class and capitalism.

not everyone has the financial privilege to be ill in peace

Big time drilla

suppressed, until I started talking about them. I started You Look Okay to Me because I was speaking to other people at university after I got diagnosed and realized how prevalent chronic illness was. You know, people go, 'Oh, I've got Crohn's, by the way.' It's just really offhand. It's clearly something that was around, but they weren't speaking about it openly. And then when I started to cover certain aspects of it, a lot of people either said, 'I didn't know this was happening. I had no idea,' or, 'Yes, exactly. More people should talk about this.' There are many

other people doing similar work. But it's being brave enough to be one of the people actually pushing.

If it weren't for conversations like this, we wouldn't be having conversations about how people with dark skin are completely misdiagnosed half the time in medicine. This was always there, but these conversations are often hidden. Ten years ago we weren't having the same conversations about invisible illness as we are now. We didn't have the 'please offer me a seat' badges. I'm not going to say, I'm the only one doing it, but being someone that has these conversations allows more people to piggyback off you. Then it spirals outwards in various ways and creates a shift or change. We're not there yet, but there's definitely a lot more visibility in the media about chronic and invisible illnesses now. It takes the work of the online community, and what I and others do, to make that change, I think.

Reuben: I think advocacy like this has brought attention to the infrastructure around disability, encouraging people to be less presumptuous about what disability is and what a disabled person looks like. I'd love to talk more about the other work you do in making visible what's obscured. I'm thinking about your work on the Black maternal health gap and also diagnosis inequality. Could you talk a little more about how you research that and the systematic inequality that you try to make visible, and how you share all of this on your platform?

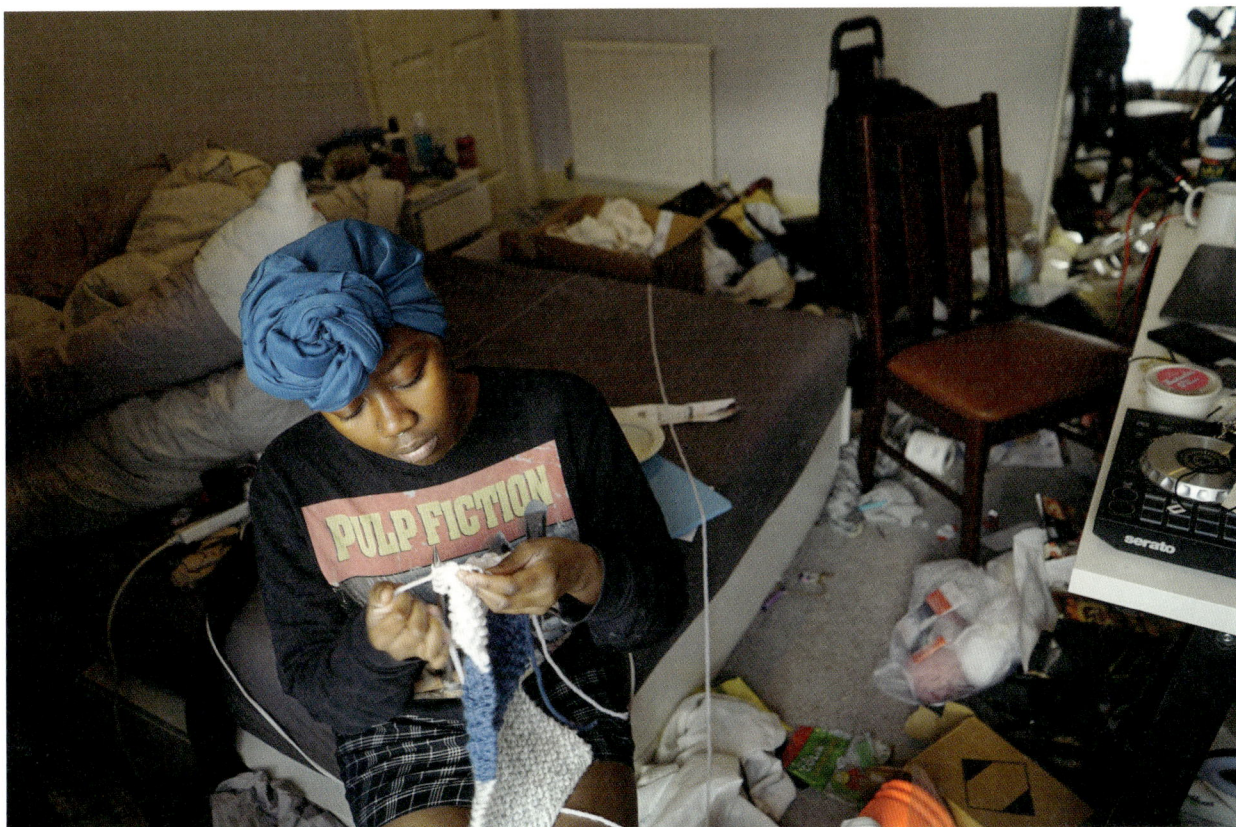

Jameisha: I try especially with my offline – the slower artwork – but also some of my online content, to speak about, some of the healthcare inequities that happen. From the point of view of Black communities, but also to amplify the voices of other groups who are talking about it, too. But, through my personal experience of dealing with medical racism specifically, it sparked a thread of realizing that there is a whole history that informs that experience.

A lot of my artwork that's offline focuses on digging for research to find ways to bring stories to light, so that it can stop. A lot of people were shocked in the film that I made on Black pain that there is an idea that Black people have a higher pain tolerance that is documented in English history. But the problem is that a lot of our research on this is American history. I'm realizing that actually it's quite invisible here, in the UK, and we don't have those conversations as often as Black Americans do, but I'm so inspired by the people who have done the work to really bring these stories to light. What exists in our history that influences the way that we're sick now? I try to make work that allows more engaging ways to have those conversations. So whether it is the Black pain gap, whether it's Black maternal mortality, all of these things come from somewhere. I try to make work that

we all deserve the
space to be ill
in peace

points to where it exists and hope that we can continue to have conversations that genuinely have an impact on people's lives. And it's something that people aren't even aware of until I tell them. They have no clue, not even doctors. But the research is there. You can find it. And one thing about England – the institutions that house this historical research, they still exist. You can go to the London School of Hygiene and Tropical Medicine today, and that's where a lot of those papers were written, you know. So it's also about holding them to account, as well.

Reuben: It's interesting, isn't it, because it's not actually like these places are invisible? These colonial institutions still exist and are still functional and powerful. It's that these things are so accepted by the people who practise medicine or who administer these systems.

One of your early works on You Look Okay to Me is a photograph of a piece of paper with your handwriting on saying, 'I've noticed a commonality in those of us living with chronic illnesses. We share a desperate need to be believed, and this feeling is not unwarranted, it is quintessential to our survival.' How do you think these networks of 'radical visibility' – the disabled and sick internet subculture begun by Sky Cubacub (see pp 116–19) – and care that we've been discussing are established on social media? When I say radical visibility I'm referring to what you said earlier about pushing against the demands

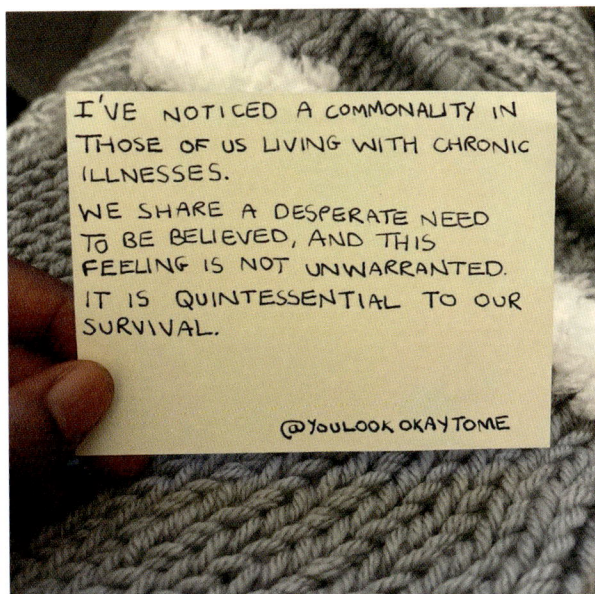

I'VE NOTICED A COMMONALITY IN THOSE OF US LIVING WITH CHRONIC ILLNESSES.

WE SHARE A DESPERATE NEED TO BE BELIEVED, AND THIS FEELING IS NOT UNWARRANTED. IT IS QUINTESSENTIAL TO OUR SURVIVAL.

@YOULOOKOKAYTOME

of capitalism in terms of how we as disabled people show up, as our fullest selves. How does You Look Okay to Me contribute to creating the conditions not only for sick and disabled people to survive, but also to thrive?

Jameisha: The networks that exist, especially on social media, like 'radical visibility', allow other sick people to say, 'Oh my God, same!' I think, without them, you internalize a lot of your experience. Now there is a network of people who are very visible with their illness and how they are treated: 'This happened to me, this is bullshit!' It makes other people think, 'I thought that was normal. I didn't think I had the right to complain,' or 'Oh my gosh. I'm gonna talk about this now.' I think we're moving away from simply surviving to thriving, knowing that we deserve more and are allowed to ask for more. You don't know until you hear

someone else say something. And I can say that for myself because, before You Look Okay to Me, I was on forums. That was what mainly existed before disablity became big on social media – forums run by older white women, usually, who are a bit like 'Yes, this is the lupus forum,' and they have a tight grip on it.

Reading people saying 'Oh, they didn't listen!' made me realize that it's not me that's the problem. And it's more visible now. There's video. Now there's content. Even people speaking to doctors and doing interviews. That's allowed people to realize they deserve more. I think there's this idea about sickness – 'Oh, well, I've got my medication, so I just need to be grateful because there are some people that don't have that,' – which is true, but you actually deserve to live a good life. It might not be the life that you thought you were going to have, but it deserves to be one that's enriching. These networks show examples of visibility – and what is possible for some people. I think that's important.

All by Jameisha Prescod: p.101: *A Safe Black Birth*, 2024, photograph (Jameisha Prescod/Wellcome), p.102: *I'm disabled is the phrase that set me free*, 2021, photograph; p.103: *Lockdown*, 2021, stills; p.106: *Illness, Disability, Class & Capitalism*, 2024, video (Instagram reel); p.107: *Untangling*, 2021, photograph; Facing page, top: 'We all deserve the space to be ill in peace', 2023, Instagram post; Facing page, middle: *On Black Pain*, 2022, still; Facing page, bottom: *22 April, 2020*, still; Above: 'Being believed is quintessential to our survival', 2021, Instagram post

How to Dress Well

Essay by Ben Barry

For years, disabled people have had few choices when it comes to dressing on their own terms and in their own style. But now designers – many disabled themselves – have changed the conversation. How does what we wear reflect and represent our experiences as disabled people? In this chapter, Dr Ben Barry explores the aesthetic possibilities and sartorial nuances in designing clothes that affirm and uplift disabled life.

Right: Draped in twisting electric blue and magenta fabric chains, Sky Cubacub of Rebirth Garments radiates defiance in a shimmering headpiece and bold face paint.

As Disabled people have always existed, so too Disabled people have always been dressed. We have long hacked and altered clothing because what has been designed by the fashion industry has mostly ignored the needs and desires of our bodyminds – the understanding that the body and mind are interconnected and inseparable, shaping how we experience clothing and the world.[1] Does the rustle of fabric overstimulate us? Do the pockets on the back of our trousers cause pressure sores? Do the buttons on our shirts demand a steady grip? And if we find clothing that supports our bodyminds, is it affordable, and does the style reflect the multiplicity of our identities? Too often, the answer has been no. We have, therefore, drawn upon our lived experience and creativity to generate fashion-design innovations because we understand that access to fashion is access to life. Fashion is the epidermis between our bodyminds and society, allowing us to either conform to societal standards or to question, challenge and reimagine them. It is through dress that we can survive, navigate and thrive in our bodyminds and in the world.

As a Disabled person with low vision and as a fashion-design educator, my own experience has – by necessity – pushed me to expand fashion's emphasis on visual impact. I feel pleasure when I trace my fingers along my sequined tracksuits, producing a tactile and auditory rhythm, or each time I loop my fingers around the fringe of my university robe, grounding myself during a lengthy convocation ceremony. My teaching and research embrace this disability-first understanding of fashion and raise critical questions about who, among us as Disabled people, truly has access to fashion and what it means to be granted access. I recognize that my relationship to fashion is shaped by significant privilege. My whiteness, thinness, cisgender identity, non-apparent disability and financial security grant me access to clothing and the freedom to dress in almost any way I choose. For Disabled people whose bodyminds do not align with these privileges – those who are racialized, trans, fat and/or apparently Disabled – and who face financial precarity, the relationship between dress and disability is far more complex.

There is a tension involved in 'dressing well' as Disabled. I understand 'dressing well' not as an aesthetic dictated by the

Above: A 1958 Functional Fashions catalogue featuring models highlighting the accessibility features of a wrap dress and trousers.

runways of New York, London or Tokyo, but rather as having access to clothing and the agency to select garments that allow us to feel comfortable, safe and empowered – to feel at home in our bodyminds. By analyzing select pieces from fashion brands that are designed with Disabled wearers in mind, I highlight how dressing as Disabled often involves oscillating between assimilating into non-Disabled cultures and embracing, even accentuating, our Disabled bodyminds. Our everyday dress strategies require careful negotiation of the joys, risks, benefits and pressures of fashioning our bodyminds in and for the social world. This process is shaped by our proximity to non-Disabled standards and in relation to the other intersecting layers of our identities. Yet the freedom to dress well is not equally extended in the disability community. Ableism – a system of discrimination and prejudice that favours non-Disabled norms – exerts pressure both externally, through cultural and societal expectations, and internally, as Disabled people often feel compelled to assimilate into these standards. The dynamic influences many fashion designers, both Disabled and non-Disabled, to create clothing that aligns with non-Disabled culture. As a result hierarchies are reinforced not only between Disabled and non-Disabled people but also within Disabled communities themselves, where some of us enjoy far greater access and freedom than others in the pursuit of dressing well.

The fashion industry has coined various monikers to categorize clothing designed specifically for Disabled wearers, ranging from 'accessible' to 'inclusive' fashion to the more common 'adaptive fashion'. While these labels help Disabled wearers identify clothing that might meet their needs, the design ideologies and practices underpinning them often reinforce the belief that Disabled people's clothing should facilitate their integration into non-Disabled dress culture. Even the term 'adaptive fashion' implies that non-Disabled bodyminds are the standard from which designers must retrofit – adapt – clothing for Disabled wearers. By framing Disabled bodyminds as deviations from the presumed norm, adaptive fashion perpetuates a hierarchical divide between Disabled and non-Disabled dressed bodyminds. Its underlying premise suggests that clothing must be adapted to 'fit' our bodyminds because, to heed disability scholar Rosemarie Garland-Thomson, we otherwise 'misfit' into the design of fashion.[2]

Many adaptive fashion brands provide wearers with the option to assimilate into non-Disabled culture by dressing in dominant styles. One of the first mass-produced adaptive clothing lines was Functional Fashions, created by designer Helen Cookman, who was deaf, and *New York Times* style editor Virginia Pope. In a 1975 collaboration, Levi's produced a pair of jeans based on Cookman's patented design, *Trousers for a Handicapped Person*, featuring zippers down both legs and a belt to secure the front while the seat unzipped for easier bathroom

113

access. The design offered access for at least some Disabled wearers while also incorporating the then-trendy flare style. Disabled individuals, such as columnist Terry Brickley, celebrated that, 'People in wheelchairs or on crutches are now able to join the jeans generation.'[3] For Disabled people long excluded from trendy clothing, the line offered an opportunity to participate in fashion culture – provided they could afford it. While such participation reinforced conformity to non-Disabled dress norms, there is an undeniable excitement and sense of freedom in finally gaining access to the same mainstream styles that non-Disabled people have always enjoyed, particularly after a lifetime of exclusion due to limited fashion-design options.

Many adaptive fashion brands today conceal the design features that provide access for Disabled wearers – a choice that aligns with the preferences of some, but not all, wearers. UK-based UnHidden, founded by Victoria Jenkins after her own experience with chronic illnesses, offers shirts with hidden snap openings along the sleeves and down the front to allow for easy access to arm ports and stoma bags. Similarly, Dawn Adaptive in Malaysia, founded by Usha Nair based on her experience of scoliosis and that of her family, integrates discreet magnet closures inside their Magnetic Polo Tee while displaying circular buttons on its exterior. The shirt's product description on the brand website claims, 'Because there are still regular buttons on the outside, it looks like you're wearing another common T-shirt.' By hiding snaps, magnets and other accessible design elements, these brands encourage Disabled wearers to blend into non-Disabled fashion rather than celebrate the creative possibilities that disability brings to design. However, concealing clothing's access features and conforming to non-Disabled dress norms can provide emotional comfort for some Disabled wearers while also facilitating smoother visual integration into an ableist society. These garments can offer genuine benefits, particularly for Disabled people with apparent disabilities and multiply marginalized identities, by helping secure employment, increasing comfort at social gatherings and offering protection from harassment and violence in public spaces. By mirroring non-Disabled clothing aesthetics, these designs enable our dressed bodyminds to meet societal dress expectations, potentially mitigating intrusive questions about our disabilities and reducing ableist assumptions.

The design of adaptive garments often prioritizes enabling as much independent dressing as possible. Slick Chicks is a New York-based underwear brand started by Helya Mohammadian after witnessing her sister's experiences with dressing while recovering from surgery. Mohammadian designed a bra with overlapping front panels that fasten with Velcro, making it easier for wearers with limited mobility and dexterity to dress themselves. While such designs can empower those who have previously relied on assistance due to the limitations of ableist clothing designs, these items may also reinforce the assumption that dependency inherently compromises personal privacy and dignity. Underlying this perspective is the myth that independent personhood is always preferable to interdependence – a reality for many Disabled people regardless of clothing design. Interdependence is a cornerstone of the systems of care and mutual aid of disability culture that honour collective well-being over individualism and demonstrate that reliance on others is not a weakness but a source of creativity and community. It is a delicate balance, yet both can be true: dress features that facilitate independent dressing can offer greater autonomy to some Disabled wearers while also reflecting and potentially reinforcing a broader cultural bias that prioritizes independence as a universal ideal.

Adaptive fashion brands often design clothing to bring Disabled wearers closer to approximating non-Disabled body ideals. Kathy D. Woods founded KDW, her eponymous womenswear label for Little People, after a lifetime of struggling to find clothing that expressed her style and fitted her body. Inspired by Diane von Furstenberg's iconic wrap dress, Woods's designs emphasize a lean, elongated silhouette – a gendered body ideal that dominates fashion culture. As Woods explains in an interview with *The Washington Post* in 2015, her pieces are 'not going to make you look wide, or much

bigger than you really are, and [are] something that will give you length'.[4] While these designs might appear to conform to feminine beauty ideals, Woods's work must be understood within the context of her identities as a Black Disabled woman in the USA – two communities historically excluded from dominant feminine beauty ideals and fashionable representations due to anti-Black racism and ableism. For Woods and her clients, embracing these silhouettes is a radical and joyful act of self-representation within a fashion

Above: Three vibrant Rebirth Garments ensembles with bold cutouts, geometric accessories, and layered textures in vivid pinks, purples and blues.

their bodyminds, envision new political and social possibilities and build disability worlds. Grounded in their disability and queer experience, Sky Cubacub founded Rebirth Garments, a Chicago-based brand that designs size-inclusive and gender-nonconforming clothing. Cubacub's fashion philosophy celebrates 'radical visibility' by incorporating bold geometric patterns, contrasting colours and revealing cuts to encourage wearers to highlight parts of their Disabled, fat, queer and trans bodyminds that society stigmatizes and shuns. For example, Rebirth Garments's Holster Pouch is designed to allow wearers to hold the Krypton MVP machine – a portable air-disinfecting device – while transforming its sterile design into a vibrant fashion accessory. Available in neon green, pastel pink and bright yellow, the vinyl pouch features versatile loops that allow it to be attached to a belt or harness or even worn as a necklace by adding rings. As Cubacub writes in their 'Radical Visibility: A QueerCrip Dress Reform Movement Manifesto', 'In the face of what society tells us to hide, we are unapologetic individuals who want to celebrate and highlight our bodies.'[5]

system that has excluded them. There is also an affirming comfort for Disabled people whose bodies have always stood out as *extraordinary* to simply dress *ordinary*, adhering to the conventions of fashionable femininity in this case. Simultaneously, as Little People, Woods and her clients can never fully satisfy non-Disabled feminine beauty standards. Instead, they reinterpret these ideals on their own terms, centring their own bodies and experiences within these aesthetics.

Some designers take a more radical approach by creating fashion that encourages Disabled wearers to amplify

Above: An ear adorned with DeafMetal jewellery, where gold and pearl-accented chains elegantly connect a hearing aid to decorative earrings.

Other fashion designers embrace disability as an aesthetic opening for new shapes, textiles and sensory engagements. These designers often celebrate the aesthetic possibilities of access features, rather than minimizing them. Finnish accessories designer Jenni Ahtiainen, for example, after being fitted for her first hearing aids decided to transform the sterile device into a bold fashion accessory. Her brand, DeafMetal Hearing Aid Jewelry, creates jewellery that attaches to hearing aids, accentuating them as expressions of style and identity. Similarly, Canadian Bronwyn Berg and her disabled partner Hal Bennett designed spikes to fasten onto the back handles of Berg's wheelchair following an incident when a stranger pushed her without consent. The spikes offer Berg, as a Disabled woman, a sense of physical and psychological safety in public by deterring unsolicited physical contact. The spikes also expand the aesthetic possibilities of wheelchair handles, challenge the ableist assumption that Disabled people depend on charity from non-Disabled individuals, and encourage dialogue about the importance of seeking consent before offering assistance to a Disabled person.

Still other fashion designers embrace disability as the *starting* point in design, rather than adapting existing designs originally created for non-Disabled wearers. Sugandha Gupta, a blind textiles designer in New York, developed 'sensory textiles' using a variety of techniques for manipulating fabrics – including embroidery, crochet and felting – to create tactile, wearable pieces that can be experienced through sight, sound, touch, taste and smell. Her tactile felted wearable piece is a reversible scarf-like accessory with two distinct textures: one side is a sculptural bubble-like structure, with different materials inside each bubble, including

beads, cotton balls or fibre, and the other side is soft and cushioned. Wearers experience various sensations as different parts of the piece touch their neck and shoulders.

Recognizing the balance between assimilating into non-Disabled culture and embracing Disabled fashion culture, some fashion designers offer a middle ground. Cool Crutches, co-founded by Amelia Peckham (with Clare Braddell)

Above: Sugandha Gupta's tactile felted wearable piece can be worn around the neck and shoulder.

following her spinal-cord injury, produce walking sticks and crutches in bold patterns and colours, such as the vibrant jewel tones of gold and green. At the same time Cool Crutches market their products as silent, avoiding the rattling sounds that most mobility aids make. Peckham's experience with crutches inspired the silent design, as she explained in an interview with *Hello!* in 2024: 'The clicking made me so self-conscious. I could never go anywhere without someone hearing me.'[6]

Dressing as Disabled is a constant navigation. Disabled people have most commonly been offered adaptive clothing and accessories that *minimize*

Above: Amelia Peckham, co-founder of Cool Crutches, stands beside a row of vibrantly patterned walking sticks designed for both style and silent mobility.

our experiences of disability and *reduce* disability as dressed markers of difference. Intentionally or not, these designs align with the medical model of disability by presenting fashion as a 'solution' to manage our individual bodyminds and the social stigma of living in an ableist society. The underlying message is that we should feel ashamed of our disabilities and use clothing to mitigate both our insecurity and others' discrimination. In contrast, other designers embrace disability as a creative, imaginative and generative force in fashion. Their designs align clearly with 'crip', a reclamation of a historically pejorative term by some disability activists, artists and academics, including Sky Cubacub and their visionary *QueerCrip Manifesto*. Crip is both a political stance and celebratory identity, similar to the reclamation of the term queer.

While crip remains contested within the disability community due to its complex history, for those of us who proudly use it, it represents an active rejection of the idea of disability as something to be fixed or assimilated into the norm. Rather, crip desires disability as 'a valuable cultural identity, a source of knowledge, and a basis for relationality.'[7] In fashion, designers and wearers who claim crip turn away from non-Disabled fashion culture and instead create one uniquely our own.

For many Disabled wearers the choice between sartorial conformity and radical visibility is complicated and, more often than not, beyond our control. Embracing a colourful, clicking walking stick can be a bold declaration of disability pride – a loud, vibrating chorus announcing a Disabled person's arrival and a visual tool to confront ableist stares. Still, it can also limit our access to professional and social opportunities, increase the risk of surveillance and scrutiny, and exacerbate disability stigma. Claiming disability through dress may also require us to expend even more energy just to navigate the world. Constantly confronting inaccessible environments and discriminatory attitudes, particularly for those who are queer, trans and/ or people of colour, is profoundly exhausting. In such contexts, preserving energy becomes a matter of survival, and clothing that conforms to accepted dress norms can offer a necessary respite from relentless ableist scrutiny. The choice of how to dress well is deeply personal and often strategic; it requires trade-offs and is always shared by systemic forces, reflecting the intersecting realities of our identities, Disabled bodyminds, finances and social contexts.

Many of the designers I have highlighted are themselves Disabled. While Disabled people are often only relegated to passive roles in the fashion-design process – as research subjects during ideation or testers during prototyping – these designers exemplify the dialogue and innovation that emerges when Disabled designers lead the fashion industry. Their work underscores the critical truth that fashion's creativity flourishes when Disabled people are fully represented as fashion designers and professionals, who are granted the credit, compensation and career pathways we deserve. These attributes, so often absent when Disabled people are only included transactionally in the fashion-design process, are essential to building a truly inclusive field. Fashion, ultimately, is not merely about designing clothing: it is a powerful force for cultural transformation. By increasing the number of Disabled fashion designers, we can cultivate new narratives and practices that educate others about disability and challenge ableist attitudes. Only when disability is valued for the beauty, wisdom and creativity that it brings to the world will Disabled people have the freedom to dress as we choose – in accordance with the plurality of our own Disabled experiences, identities, desires and worlds. This is the future of fashion we must create.

How to Start a Studio

In this chapter Intoart co-founders Ella Ritchie and Sam Jones speak with artists and designers Clifton Wright and Nancy Clayton about the Intoart studio. Illustrated design journeys offer insight into the signature style of studio artist Andre Williams' interior design and Ntiense Eno-Amooquaye's fashion design.

Formed in 2000 in south London, Intoart is a multi-disciplinary art, design and craft studio which operates as an evolving alternative art school and pioneering studio programme to champion the equity, leadership and visibility of learning disabled and autistic artists, designers and makers. Working across a wide range of media, the Intoart studio is a site of ambitious art, design and craft production leading to exhibitions, commissions, collaborations and publishing.

Nancy Clayton
artist, designer and Intoart studio member
Sam Jones
programme director and co-founder of Intoart
Ella Ritchie
director and co-founder of Intoart
Clifton Wright
artist, designer and Intoart studio member

SJ: When we were asked 'How do you create a studio?' we decided that the best way to answer the question would be collectively, because our studio is about shared experiences.

CW: What was it like getting Intoart started?

ER: Intoart started as a small project, initially over 12 weeks with just eight people, soon after we had graduated art college. We worked with community and youth workers and a gallery, in parallel. It was really important to us to work with people who had specialist skill sets to organize and make the projects happen. That was the difference about Intoart at that time – how we made those different roles work together. Bringing our experience of art practice, we were working with organizations with skills and experience in supporting people to integrate a vision of social justice and art practice and to build a studio.

NC: Art can change society. If you've got a good imagination then art can be powerful. In your imagination and in

Christian Ovonlen at the Intoart studio

121

society. I think we've still got a long way to go but I can see us being included more as human beings and artists.

CW: I want to be known as Clifton Wright the artist.

NC: I'm kind of in between – I think it's important to talk about disability as well, but sometimes I feel like I just want to be called by my name, Nancy.

SJ: Clifton, what was your first experience of Intoart?

CW: When I started I didn't think I would make it past day one – but here I am, 20 years later. It makes me wonder about the difference between what I was doing

Above left: Clifton Wright, *Borrowed Picasso Portrait*, pastel on paper, 2017

Above right: Nancy Clayton, *Live in a New World*, acrylic and pastel on cotton, 2024

back then and what I am doing now in the studio.

ER: Had you made art before?

CW: Well, if you can call papier-mâché plates art, but that's about it really.

ER: So, you didn't know what to expect then? What made you come back?

CW: Using more materials and seeing where it can go. Drawing helps you do something with your life. Plus, it gives you something to achieve. It makes you busy because of the hard work.

ER: What about you, Nancy, what are your earliest experiences?

NC: It was hard finding myself when growing up … and what I wanted to do. In my early twenties, I was a bit lost. If you go to a local college, they don't care about you that much, and your artwork.

122

I feel like they are just on 'level one'. The education system doesn't really care about you.

CW: When I think of the education system, I remember when I went to the local college to do an IT course. I was too advanced for them – not trying to brag or anything, but I was too advanced. Like you were saying, Nancy, about 'level one'.

ER: There are so many structural barriers for learning disabled people to access higher education and, therefore, art school. Art school is traditionally the route people take to learn about the visual arts, to form peer groups and networks that can take them into a career as an artist or designer. So Intoart provides an alternative art-school experience for learning disabled people.

NC: Art is finding my own journey and, also, to me, an education. Education is important to me.

ER: The education point is a relevant one, Nancy, in terms of where Intoart started. We felt that learning disabled people didn't have the same opportunities that we had at art school which is why we started Intoart. When Sam and I were at Central Saint Martins doing fine art, we could do screen-printing, etching, lithography, and go to the sculpture, painting or film department. I could go to the equipment store and book out what I needed. During my time at art school, I started working with learning disabled people in a community setting. I was given pens that didn't quite work and sugar paper – which definitely were not equal to the materials and learning I had access to. We started Intoart because there wasn't really anything like it. We felt it was important that there wasn't only a space to make art but also a space to learn about art. We wanted to address how you develop an art school with learning disabled people that meets needs across a spectrum of access points and with high aspirations.

SJ: We valued our art education and when you value something you want to share it and also to sustain it somehow. To carry on having that relationship to art and creativity, it can have a big impact on how you think about yourself, what you can achieve. That's what's special about Intoart the aim is to go on and on, and to build a community.

NC: Yeah, I think art is power. Expectations of what Disabled people can achieve are higher at Intoart. It's more a specialist organization and about being professional. At Intoart we are pushing to the next level, creating opportunities and success, and winning prizes for our generation and the next – making sure our voices are heard. I feel like I'm nearly there with what I want to do, which is creativity and collaboration.

CW: Yeah, the sky is the limit. The world is your oyster.

NC: In the studio we talk about our ideas, our work. We plan collaborations, travel, think about art and culture and opportunities. We all want to achieve something, to have challenges and experiences. To have confidence.

ER: I remember, in a film you made in 2009 for an Intoart exhibition at the Whitechapel Gallery, Clifton, you said one of the things you wanted to do was travel to a different country. One of the important things about the studio is hearing where people want to go – their aspirations – and helping bring that about.

CW: For me it's a mix of looking at art and making art: visiting Dulwich Picture Gallery to look at Canaletto and then planning a trip to Venice; going on a gondola and looking at painters like Tintoretto, Titian and Veronese. Borrowing other artists' work, like Picasso did, and elevating it.

ER: You made a whole body of work about Picasso's portraits, and then your drawing, *Borrowed Picasso*, was exhibited at the Drawing Room gallery's exhibition *Drawn Portraits* in 2018, next to *Tête* (1943) by Picasso himself. Do you think that challenges people's perceptions of who can be an artist?

CW: Anyone can be an artist, no matter what background you've got.

ER: That's what's always been important – that the work you are making in the studio creates opportunities. The artists and designers are creating the opportunities through their work. What do you think Intoart's role is in that?

NC: I feel like my journey at Intoart is about speaking my language and finding my own voice. I just feel so grateful for all the equipment and materials around us in the studio. The magic of the studio is just having fun, being creative, being kind to one another, being respectful. Caring about people and the equipment and materials.

CW: Having the responsibility to decide what paper, what materials and how big. Even working with [handmade paper mill] the Paper Foundation in the Lake District, I made my own coloured papers, which I am using in a new 11-metre (36-ft) wide drawing I'm working on in the studio.

ER: That is the magic that people pick up on – looking from the outside at the work that's being made in the studio. That attention to detail. Every artist has their own language – it isn't just one pot of materials that everyone dips into. It's very bespoke which materials artists choose and how they want to use them. Artists push the boundaries of those materials in the studio. Clifton, you mix up your materials in lots of different ways – some of that is classical, technical ways of working. Then sometimes it's 'Let's see what happens when I mix those things,' and an explosive language emerges.

SJ: To describe how we are experiencing 'making' in the Intoart studio – would you say it's a kind of swimming pool, and you just jump in?

CW: Yeah, sink or swim!

SJ: So immersive learning, using loads of different materials, looking at a wide range of art, design and craft, and allowing the artist to emerge. Experiencing work in exhibitions, through travel and always making your own work. Taking time to experience and try things out and deciding what you like, step by step.

CW: When I am at home, I still think about what I have been doing in the studio. I just get into it. As time goes on – it's nearly 20 years now since I first came to Intoart – I feel like art is a part of me. I want to talk about the different materials and techniques in my work and to take things to another level. I want to be seen as an artist who pushes the envelope to talk about the past and the present and the future all at the same time. As a contemporary artist not an outsider artist.

ER: I wonder whether Intoart is a useful collective voice, because we can say that Intoart is the sum of all this lived experience. Clifton, you can go out and do your thing but still say 'I am part of something', where there is this shared collective belief in social justice and equity, to challenge ableism and stigma. Someone might come into the studio and share that they have had a bad experience that week. We're not going to share those personal stories, but collectively they develop a story about what it means to live in a society where it is challenging if you are a Disabled person.

SJ: And maybe, when it's a collective voice,

people aren't isolated in the same way as when the focus is on a personal history.

NC: Yes, I think so.

ER: There is a strength and power in a collective of different voices.

CW: In terms of people's perceptions, when we were nominated for the Hublot Design Prize (which supports and highlights up-and-coming designers), in 2023, I felt like we were pushing the boundaries, being included with other up-and-coming designers from all over the world.

ER: So some people just don't expect the things we do to happen?

CW: Yes, but when you find something that you're passionate about then just go for it. No matter what other people think you can or cannot do.

SJ: There is an energy in the studio about pushing forward – a positive energy that pushes at boundaries and preconceptions.

NC: For me it's about working with the right people, who enjoy your work, and breaking boundaries together.

ER: Sometimes it is quite straight-forward, finding people that want to work together and just getting on with it, step by step. Jumping in the swimming pool together!

SJ: Do you both feel that you are part of

a history of art, design and creativity?

CW: Yes, I do. I've been in exhibitions with artists that are living, like David Hockney, Dryden Goodwyn, Melanie Jackson, and also no longer with us – Maria Lassnig, Frank Auerbach and Paula Rego. I have different ways and methods of drawing that fit into a history of art.

NC: I feel like I am part of Intoart history, but not in the art world yet.

ER: There is a difference, Nancy, between what you feel is your space and your way of doing things and the established consensus about what art, design and craft are. There are so many moments where the work people have made has changed the direction of what we do. The work of Andre Williams, his graphic style and use of colour and typography, led to the founding of our design studio, Trifle Studio. Our craft studio has come out of the work that you, Clifton, with Christian Ovonlen and Mawuena Kattah, were making in textiles and ceramics. We haven't built those programmes because me and Sam sat in a room and thought, 'That's what we're going to do.' It all comes out of the work that is made and the ideas that are made, and that's what's exciting for us.

NC: Yeah, I'm seeing where it leads.

Intoart Design Journeys

Design practice is integral to the Intoart studio, impacting on the work produced by individual artists and designers for exhibition and publishing as well as leading to collaborations and commissions.

Design is a process for expanding visual language and application for artists working in the Intoart studio. Works emerge from the artist's own practice as well as from externally commissioned projects and collaborations. Examples include Andre Williams who creates bespoke interior design and public-realm sculpture and Ntiense Eno-Amooquaye who produces couture fashion collections, film, photography and performance.

Below: Maweuna Kattah, *Aunty, Mum and Me Talking About My Fabric Collection*, 2016

Andre Williams: Design Journey

Andre Williams' *Hidden Room*, 2023, is an installation of handcrafted furniture, textiles and ceramics. Williams explains: 'I turn small drawings into big projects and fill spaces with colour. I want people who see my work to smile and laugh and have their own new ideas.'

Concept The forest floor as an endlessly interesting but potentially dangerous place with hidden snakes, poisonous frogs and creepy crawlies.

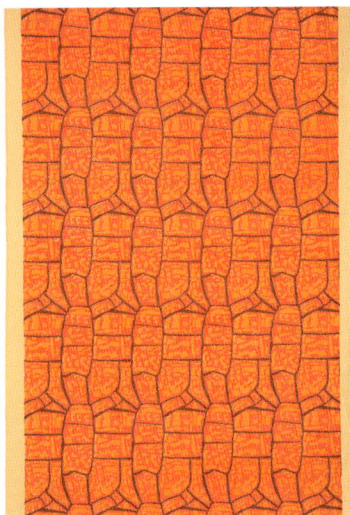

Drawing: Design for Turtle Chair, one of many ideas for building a room. The chair is the centrepiece for sitting in the Hidden Room installation, alongside the Blues Bookshelf and Tripod Table.

Pattern: Turtle-shell textile design. Layered monochrome drawings are tiled into a repeat-pattern design for textile. Hand screen-printed on linen for interior applications.

Making: Furniture produced from the drawing is made into 3-dimensional form. Turned and vectored silhouettes create the wooden frame made in collaboration with the timber workshop at The Exchange, Erith, in southeast London. Frame hand painted by the artist with plump upholstering using printed textile to form the effect of a turtle shell.

**Ntiense Eno-Amooquaye:
Design Journey**

Concept: *Nation, Rocking
on the Edge* is one of nine
dresses designed and
modelled by the artist for her
exhibition *Crashing the Glass
Slippers* (Chapter, Cardiff,
2024) The exhibition presented
the dresses alongside
film, photography and
performance by the artist.

Eno-Amooquaye explains of
her process: 'Design means
having different collaborations
to create new experiences.
I select a variety of drawings
that create the vibe and
atmosphere – the garment
as a new memory. Seeing my
designs on the catwalk or
exhibition with an audience is
like seeing new words and new
phrases being spoken.'

Nation, Rocking on the Edge,
2024. Worn and embodied
by the artist, fashion
design becomes a portal of
transformation. Realized
for performance, film and
photography by Ntiense
Eno-Amooquaye.

Pattern: Hand-drawn kaleidoscopic patterns taken into textile prints.

Drawing: Design for *Nation, Rocking on the Edge*, one of nine final designs referencing historic costume and avant-garde couture.

Making: Pattern cutting and construction guided by the vision and design for each iconic look. Produced in collaboration with specialist fashion and textiles practitioners.

129

Notes

Introduction

1. 'What is the social model of disability?' https://www.shapearts.org.uk/news/text-and-audio-social-model (accessed 10 April 2025)

2. R. Garland-Thomson, 'Misfits: A Feminist Materialist Disability Concept', *Hypatia*, vol. 26, no. 3 (Summer 2011)

3. A. Shew, *Against Technoableism: Rethinking Who Needs Improvement* (New York 2024)

4. A. Shew, 'Technological Knowledge in Disability Design' in Andrew Wells Garnar and A. Shew, *Feedback Loops* (Lanham 2020)

5. L. Jackson, A. Haagard, R. Williams, 'Disability Dongle', *Platypus*, https://blog.castac.org/2022/04/disability-dongle/ (19 April 2022, accessed 8 April 2025)

6. T. Siebers, *Disability Aesthetics* (Ann Arbor 2020)

7. E. Guffey, *After Universal Design* (London 2023).

8. https://sinsinvalid.org/10-principles-of-disability-justice/ (accessed 2 April 2025)

9. Govt of Japan city apologizes after bus driver refuses disabled man's boarding using app, https://mainichi.jp/english/articles/20240829/p2a/00m/0na/026000c (accessed 2 April 2025)

10. Wheelchair Users Block the Seoul Subway as the Right Takes Power, https://www.thenation.com/article/world/korea-disability-protest/ (accessed 2 April 2025)

11. J. White-Johnson, 'The Anti Ableist Art Educators Manifesto', https://jenwhitejohnson.com/The-Anti-Ableist-Art-Educators-Manifesto (2022; accessed 2 April 2025)

12. R. Chapman, *Empire of Normality* (London 2003)

5: How to Design a Neighbourhood

1. https://www.e-flux.com/architecture/positions/624965/outline-for-a-disability-critique-of-property/ (October 2024; accessed 2 April 2025)

2. Cody Burchfield, Isabella Teran, Ariana Contreras, Cameron Gillern, Fatema Mostafa, Genevieve Zanaska, Lina Kudinar, and Nicole Kuo.

3. https://www.centerforarchitecture.org/video/block-party-from-independent-living-to-disability-communalism/ (July 2022; accessed 2 April 2025)

4. Ibid.

5. Ibid.

6. Maya Tulip Lorey, 'A History of Residential Segregation in Berkeley, California, 1878–1960', The Concord Review 24, no. 2 (2014), pp.1-19

7. See note 1

7: How to Protest

1. https://marcgarrett.org/2014/02/12/diwo-do-it-with-others-artistic-co-creation-as-a-decentralized-method-of-peer-empowerment-in-todays-multitude/ (Feb 2014; accessed 2 April 2025)

2. https://bmjopen.bmj.com/content/7/11/e017722 (November 2017; accessed 2 April 2025)

3. https://jech.bmj.com/content/76/12/1027 (November 2022; accessed 2 April 2025)

4. https://immerse.news/public-by-proxy-244940a22981 (March 2021; accessed 2 April 2025)

5. https://leavingevidence.wordpress.com/2011/05/05/access-intimacy-the-missing-link/ (May 2011; accessed 2 April 2025)

6. https://accesspowervisibility.com (accessed 2 April 2025)

7. https://rebirthgarments.com/radical-visibility-zine (accessed 2 April 2025)

9: How to Dress Well

1. Bodymind is a term developed and used by disability scholars including Eli Clare, Margaret Price and Sami Schalk.

2. Rosemarie Garland-Thomson, 'Misfits: A Feminist Materialist Disability Concept', *Hypatia*, vol. 26, no. 3 (Summer 2011), pp.591–609

3. The Washington Post, 18 February 2015

4. Tracey Panek, 'Levi's® – An Early Adopter of Functional Fashion', Levi Strauss & Co, https://www.levistrauss.com/2019/04/10/levis-an-early-adopter-of-functional-fashion (April 2019, accessed 5 December 2024)

5. Sky Cubacub, 'Radical Visibility: A QueerCrip Dress Reform Movement Manifesto', https://rebirthgarments.com/radical-visibility-zine (October 2019, accessed 10 December 2024)

6. *Hello!* 30 May 2024

7. Aimi Haraie, *Building Access: Universal Design and the Politics of Disability*, (Minneapolis 2017), p.12

Further Reading

Architecture and Urban Design

- Jos Boys, *Disability, Space, Architecture: A Reader* (London 2017)
- David Gissen, *The Architecture of Disability: Buildings, Cities, and Landscapes Beyond Access* (Minnesota 2022)
- The Disordinary Architecture Project, *Many More Parts Than M!* (London 2024; online at https://disordinaryarchitecture. co.uk/start-learning/many-more-parts)
- Aimi Hamraie, *Building Access: Universal Design and the Politics of Disability* (Minnesota 2019)
- Sara Hendren, *What Can a Body Do? How We Meet the Built World* (New York 2020)
- Lezlie Lowe, *No Place to Go: How Public Toilets Fail Our Private Needs* (London 2018)

Design

- Sasha Constanza-Chock, *Design Justice: Community-Led Practices to Build the Worlds We Need* (Cambridge, MA 2020)
- Arseli Dokumacı, *Activist Affordances: How Disabled People Improvise More Habitable Worlds* (Durham, NC 2023)
- Elizabeth Guffey, *After Universal Design: The Disability Design Revolution* (London 2023)
- Elizabeth Guffey and Bess Williamson, *Making Disability Modern: Design Histories* (London 2020)
- Liz Jackson, 'We Are the Original Lifehackers', *New York Times*, 30 May 2018
- Ellen Lupton, Farah Kafei, Jennifer Tobias et al., *Extra Bold: A Feminist, Inclusive, Anti-racist, Nonbinary Field Guide for Graphic Designers* (Princeton 2021)

- Mara Mills and Rebecca Sanchez, *Crip Authorship – Disability as Method* (New York 2023)
- Ashley Shew, *Against Technoableism: Rethinking Who Needs Improvement* (New York 2023)
- Jaipreet Virdi, *Hearing Happiness* (Chicago 2020)

Fashion and Textiles

- Gill Crawshaw, *Rights Not Charity: Protest Textiles and Disability Activism* (London 2023)
- Kate Annett-Hitchcock, *The Intersection of Fashion and Disability: a Historical Analysis* (London 2023)
- Grace Jun, *Fashion, Disability, and Co-design: a Human-centered Design Approach* (London 2024)
- Natalie E. Wright '"Functional Fashions for the Physically Handicapped": Disability and Dress in Postwar America', *The Journal of the Costume Society of America*, vol. 48, August 2022

Politics, History and Culture

- Robert Chapman, *Empire of Normality, Neurodiversity and Capitalism* (London 2023)
- Rachel Charlton-Dailey, *Ramping Up Rights: An Unfinished History of British Disability Activism* (London 2025)
- Anushay Hossain, *The Pain Gap: How Sexism and Racism in Healthcare Kill Women* (London 2021)
- Jasbir K. Puar, *Right to Maim: Debility, Capacity, Disability* (Durham, NC 2017)
- Marta Russell, *Capitalism and Disability* (Chicago 2021)

- Frances Ryan, *Crippled: Austerity and the Demonization of Disabled People* (London 2019)
- Sami Schalk, *Black Disability Politics* (Durham, NC 2022)
- Artie Vierkant and Beatrice Adler-Bolton, *Health Communism* (London 2022)
- *Crip Camp* (documentary), James Lebrecht and Nicole Newnham (dirs) (Higher Ground Productions 2020)

Disability Theory and Experience

- H-Dirksen L. Bauman and Joseph J. Murray (eds), *Deaf Gain: Raising the Stakes for Human Diversity* (Minneapolis 2014)
- Johanna Hedva, *Sick Woman Theory* (Iowa 2020)
- Alison Kafer, *Feminist, Queer, Crip* (Indiana 2013)
- Robert McRuer, *Crip Theory: Cultural Signs of Queerness and Disability* (New York 2006)
- Tom Shakespeare, *Disability: The Basics* (London 2017)
- Tobin Siebers, *Disability Aesthetics* (Michigan 2010)
- Alice Wong, *Disability Visibility* (New York 2020)

Creative Practice

- Sonia Boue, *Neurophototherapy* (Self published 2023)
- Jo Spence, *Putting Myself in the Picture: A Political, Personal and Photographic Autobiography* (London 1986)

- Shayda Kafai, *Crip Kinship: The Disability Justice & Art Activism of Sins Invalid* (Vancouver 2022)

Videogames Design

- Tama Leaver, Mike Kent, Katie Ellis (eds), *Gaming Disability: Disability Perspectives on Contemporary Video Games* (Abingdon 2022)
- Markus Spöhrer and Beate Ochsner (eds), *Disability and Video Games: Practices of En-/Disabling Modes of Digital Gaming* (London, New York and Shanghai 2024)

Glossary

Able-bodied
Able-bodied is often used as shorthand to describe someone who is not disabled. However, this phrase has been challenged by disabled communities who are also 'able-bodied' – instead offers the phrase 'non-disabled' to describe someone who is not disabled.

Ableism/Ableist
Ableism is discrimination, social prejudices and structural injustices against disabled people. Otherwise understood as the belief that non-disabled people are superior to disabled people. This is a concept like racism or sexism in the sense that it is structural and manifests in various forms, such as discrimination, stereotyping or exclusion.

Access features
Access features refer to the elements or features of a given design that enable access. Access features span a wide spectrum, for example both an easy-grip handle and a screen reader are access features.

Access intimacy
Access intimacy is a concept named and shaped by community organizer, writer, and disability justice advocate Mia Mingus. Often hard to standardize, it refers to the feeling of having your access needs genuinely understood and respected. Mingus also describes a specific kind of access intimacy shared by disabled and sick people who understand one another through their shared or similar experiences of ableism.

Accessibility
Accessibility refers to the capability of an object or subject to be reached, used and understood. In the context of disability, accessibility often refers to a design that has been adapted for use by disabled people, for example, an 'accessible toilet' would be understood to have certain design features, whereas a 'toilet' may not have or be assumed to have those features.

Acute illness
An acute illness is a short-term illness.

Adaptive
Adaptive means adapted or adaptable to the needs of disabled people.

Adaptive design
Adaptive design is adapted or adaptable by and for the needs of disabled users, and, by extension, can have advantages for other groups, such elderly people.

Adaptive fashion
Adaptive fashion is adapted or adaptable by and for the needs of disabled users.

Algorithmic hostility
Algorithmic hostility refers to the ways that algorithms reproduce and perpetuate structures of power or oppression, manifesting as hostility towards marginalized people in digital contexts, thus mirroring the conditions of the society in which the algorithm was produced. This can also be understood as algorithmic bias.

Amputee
Used to describe a person who has an amputated limb.

Anti-ableist
Active identification of and opposition to ableism. Ultimately anti-ableism seeks to end ableism and the structures that it upholds and which uphold it.

Anti-access
Anti-access is a disabled methodology for under-standing, challenging and complicating access. In the context of design, anti-access is a means of subverting and expanding how disabled design is understood, challenging dominant understandings of what 'accessible design' is and is not.

Assimilation
Referring to the process of cultural assimilation, which is the process of becoming a part or making someone become a part of a group or society.

Assistive technology
Assistive technology is an umbrella term used to describe products or systems that support and/or assist disabled people in any and all areas of their life.

Bodymind
Bodymind is a way of understanding and referring to the human body and mind as one integrated unit, rather than two separate units. This approach establishes that knowledge and wisdom are present in all parts of the body rather than isolated to the mind. This is an idea found in many cultures across the world. The term was coined by Margaret Price in 2011.

British Sign Language (BSL)
British Sign Language (BSL) is the most common form of sign language in Britain. Like all sign languages, BSL is a visual language that uses gestures, facial expression and body language as a means of communicating. BSL is not a signed version of written or spoken English and its vocabulary and syntax are different. Sign language is used mainly by people who are Deaf or have hearing impairments.

Chronic illness
A chronic illness is a long-term illness or health condition. Some chronically sick people may also describe themselves as Disabled, but others may not.

Co-design
Co-design is a participatory design approach in which all members of a design process serve as equal collaborators, including the end users. Its aim is to meet the real-world needs of those who will use that design by being meaningfully involved with the design from start to finish.

Coercive choices
Choices that are made under conditions that remove or limit autonomy.

Crip
Crip, derived from the slur 'cripple' is used by some groups of disabled people as a politically affirmative term. Like 'queer', crip reclaims, and disarms what was previously, and may still be, a harmful term. Because of this history, crip is political in its usage, intended to disrupt, shock and challenge people. Crip intentionally transforms pathology into pride and camaraderie as it forges a distinct disabled identity, grounded in challenging and transforming ableist society.

Crip theory
Crip theory is a critical framework originating in critical disability studies, feminist and queer theory, emerging from the disability rights movement of the 1960s and 1970s. Crip theory critiques ableism and structures of violence that uphold racial capitalism. Challenging societal norms around ability, identity and the body, crip theory positions disability as political – a culture and an identity – as well as a means of understanding and interacting with the world. To 'crip' something, is to challenge and disrupt it with disabled ways of thinking or doing.

Deaf Gain
Deaf Gain approaches deafness as a gain rather than a loss. In a society that approaches deafness as a deficit, the concept of Deaf Gain challenges this, emphasizing the value of deafness to Deaf and hearing communities alike. Positioning deafness as an important and unique contribution to society and culture, Deaf Gain emphasizes the benefits of Deaf experiences.

DeafSpace and Deaf Space

DeafSpace was developed at Gallaudet University in Washington DC. It is an architectural and design framework comprising principles that prioritize the needs and experiences of Deaf people. DeafSpace challenges dominant forms of design which are hearing-centred. This is different to 'Deaf Space' which is the way that Deaf people disseminate and apply knowledge around their use of space, and is inclusive of Deaf Blind and other intersecting Deaf and Disabled identities.

Decentring

To remove or challenge a position as being important, dominant or a priority.

Deficit-based approach

A perspective that approaches disability as a loss, a problem or a deficiency that should be solved, cured or fixed. This point of view is increasingly contested, as is the medical model of disability that often accompanies it.

Disability aesthetics

A concept or approach outlined by Tobin Siebers in *Disability Aesthetics* that analyzes representations of disability in art and culture, looking to where it subverts established norms such as 'harmony, integrity and beauty' to create new aesthetics.

Disability-first

A linguistic pattern, as well as a wider practice that understands disability as an important or integral part of the identity and experiences of disabled people. For example, a disability-first approach would say: 'a disabled person' rather than 'a person who is disabled'.

Disability justice

A framework for understanding the liberation of disabled people that goes beyond rights by critiquing legal systems for their limitations and their continued contributions to the oppression of disabled and other marginalized people. Disability justice draws on ideas of collective liberation, taking an intersectional approach to understanding oppression.

Disability rights

Political, social and cultural campaigns and movement(s) advocating civil rights for disabled people that are equal to those of non-disabled people within and through legal and government systems.

Do It With Others (DIWO)

A decentralized, collaborative, networked creative approach emerging from a framework created in 2006 by media-arts organization Furtherfield that emphasizes collective participation and communal ownership.

DWP (Department for Work and Pensions)

The British government department responsible for welfare, pensions and disability benefits. The DWP has been widely and continually criticized for its treatment of disabled people, among other things.

Erasure

To make invisible, ignore, or dismiss.

Exclusion

To be prevented from participating in anything. This term is often used as shorthand to describe the systemic experiences of institutional marginalization.

Gender non-conforming

Gender expression that disregards or challenges societal expectations of gender presentation (outward expression and reading of gender, read through appearance and/or behaviour) often based on sex assigned at birth.

Ideogram

A symbol that represents an idea or concept rather than a specific word or sound, often used in accessible communication methods.

Interdependence

An approach that challenges individualism, emphasizing the importance of ways of living that bring that value or utilize interconnection, mutual support and collective care.

Intersectionality

A term coined for a legal framework by Kimberlé Crenshaw that recognizes how different aspects of a person's identity may interact with and shape each other to create unique and complex experiences.

Invisible illness or non-apparent disability
An illness or disability that is not immediately visible, often known as 'invisible illness or disability'. The term 'non-apparent' is preferred by some people.

Learning difference
A term that reframes learning disabilities as variations in cognitive processing rather than deficits. This approach is intended to reject the pathologization and belittling of people with disabilities, instead recognizing that there is no correct way to understand or be in the world, only systems that tell us that there are.

Limb difference
A preferred term for people with differences in their limbs that emphasizes diversity over 'loss' or 'deficiency'.

Little People
A term that is used in both medical and identity-based contexts. Dwarfism used to refer to people who are of short stature. However, in recent years Little People has become a popular and preferred alternative for many.

Lived experience
Describing a form of knowledge and insight acquired through first-hand experiences. For example, disabled people have lived experience of ableism, or

women have lived experience of misogyny. The term emerged to combat the hierarchies of knowledge that often emphasize the academic over the personal.

Marginalized community
A community or group of people who experience the same forms of systemic oppression under hostile social, economic or political structures.

Misfit
A term defined by Rosemarie Garland-Thomson in 2011 and used in disability studies to describe the disabled experience of attempting to fit into environments designed for non-disabled people, highlighting systemic rather than individual shortcomings. By 'misfitting', disabled people generate new knowledge around objects and environments.

Neurodivergent
Someone who is neuro-divergent is a person who diverges from the neurotype that benefits from and works with the way the society they live in operates. A person with multiple different neurocognitive neurodivergences can be called 'multiply neurodivergent'.

Neurodiversity
The concept that everyone is on a neurodiversity spectrum of infinite neurocognitive

functioning. Neurodiversity refers to everyone and cannot be used to refer to a single person.

Non-disabled
A person who is not disabled.

Open-source knowledge
Information and resources that are freely available, shareable and modifiable by the public, often with multiple contributors.

Pedagogy
Methods and theories of teaching.

Progressive disability
A disability or condition that develops or changes, becoming more profound with the passage of time.

Radical accessibility
An approach to accessibility that both goes beyond basic compliance with accessibility standards and uses access work to challenge and help create a more liberated world.

Radical visibility
Defined in Sky Cubacub's 2015 *Radical Visibility Zine*, radical visibility is a concept that encourages disabled people to be unapologetically visible and present, often through fashion and dress, in opposition to ableist erasure and exclusion.

Show out
To make an effort and/or to show off.

Social model of disability

A framework for understanding how societal, political and/or economic barriers rather than medical conditions produce experiences of disability or disablement. This approach argues for systemic change that enfranchises disabled people over medical or technological 'solutions'.

Stammer

A way of speaking that affects fluency or that does not mirror dominant standards of fluency.

Stim

A popular shortening of 'stimulation', to stim is to engage in repetitive movements or actions that produce sensations. Stimming is a behaviour that helps many neurodivergent people to self-regulate. There are as many ways to stim as are there are neurodivergent people.

Systemic inequality

A system, such as capitalism, that creates the conditions in which one group of people have an unequal status in relation to other categories of people.

Systems of care

Networks of support, comprising people and communities who are engaged and invested in caring for and sustaining each other.

Tactile

Connected to or engaging the sense of touch.

Technoableism

A form of ableism that approaches disability as an issue that should be 'fixed' by technology, rather than attending to system or social issues that disabled people face.

Undesigning

An approach that recognizes the issues of dominant models of design, challenging traditional design practices by deconstructing these ideas systems.

Ben Barry is the Dean of Fashion and Joseph and Gail Gromek Professor at Parsons School of Design in New York City. He is in the *Vogue Business* '100 Innovators' list and his teaching and research examines the intersectional fashion experiences of Disabled, fat, trans and queer individuals, working collaboratively with these communities to design clothing, fashion shows, exhibitions and programmes. Together with Sinéad Burke, Ben leads the Parsons Disabled Fashion Student Program, which supports Disabled students through recruitment, scholarships, mentorship and career pathways in the fashion industry. He holds a PhD from Cambridge University.

Nancy Clayton is a dancer and visual artist whose large-scale drawings and paintings are informed by her experience and observation of the body in motion. At Copeland Gallery in 2004 she exhibited 'Live in a New World', an expanded painting installation that addresses the lack of the Disability representation in museums and galleries. Her drawings were acquired by the Government Art Collection in 2022. She joined the Intoart studio in 2019.

Conor Foran is an Irish artist and designer based in London. As a proud person who stammers, he is interested in how disability intersects with creativity and how art and design can instigate social change. He leads a collaborative and creative practice about stammering called Dysfluent.

Arjun Harrison-Mann is a designer, activist and lecturer, whose practice foregrounds the Social Model of Disability as a design provocation. He is the co-founder and co-director of former graphic and interaction design studio Studio Hyte (2013–24), one third of Access Power Visibility collective, a member of the activist group Disabled People Against Cuts and a longstanding lecturer in design at Goldsmiths University. His work has been featured by Design Indaba, Seoul Museum of Art, Serpentine Galleries, The World Transformed, Stanley Picker Gallery, Transmediale, Furtherfield Gallery, It's Nice That, Imperfect Index, Rehearsing Freedoms, Liberty Festival, Watershed, the UK Parliament and more.

Sam Jones is co-founder and Programme Director of Intoart. He works with artists in the Intoart studio developing ambitious new bodies of work leading to exhibitions, commissions and publishing as part of Intoart's public programme and with museums, galleries and collections.

Natalie D. Kane is a curator and writer based in London. They are lead curator on *Design and Disability* and Curator of Digital Design at the V&A in the Art, Architecture, Photography and Design Department. With the V&A they curated the official UK pavilion at the 2018 London Design Biennale, and the official UK pavilion at the 2019 XXII Milan Triennale, showing the work of research group Forensic Architecture. Natalie is on the Advisory Board for the Society for Computers and Law and was a 2019 recipient of an Art Fund New Collecting Award.

Christopher Laing is an architectural designer, activist, and consultant and the founder of Signstrokes and Deaf Architecture Front. He aims to foster collaboration between the Deaf community and the architectural industry, advocating for the value of Deaf perspectives in shaping spaces. He joined Haworth Tompkins in 2017 as a Part 2 architectural assistant, after studying architecture at Kingston University and interior architecture and design at the University for the Creative Arts. He completed his MA at the Royal College of Art, where his 2021 thesis was nominated for the Spatial Justice Award. His research focuses on Deaf Space and bridging the gap between Deafness and architecture.

Poppy Levison is a designer, researcher and an educator in architecture, and disability activist working across a range of fields including art, architecture and film. She draws on her lived experience as a blind woman to highlight

139

the politics of inclusive design and accessibility, as well as the creative potential of disability. She has worked with the DisOrdinary Architecture Project for several years, including on *Architecture Beyond Sight* and *Seats at the Table*.

Reuben Liebeskind is a researcher, writer and curator from East London. Their background is in visual culture, carceral studies and community engagement. They are currently an exhibition research assistant at the V&A, having previously worked on the programme team at Grand Union Gallery. Their work has been presented at the 5th International Conference for Carceral Geography and published in *Third Text*, *The Funambulist*, and *Framing the Penal Colony*.

Jameisha Prescod is an artist–filmmaker, writer and disability advocate from south London. Their work explores the intersections of disability and chronic illness with culture, identity, politics and colonialism. Jameisha is also the founder of You Look Okay to Me, the online space for chronic illness.

Ella Ritchie is co-founder and Director of Intoart. Since 2000, she has committed her practice to Intoart, nurturing its growth and ambition. She develops Intoart's organizational and artistic programmes, working with artists and partners to realise Intoart's vision for

learning disabled and autistic people as visible, equal and established artists and designers.

Emily Sara is a queer, disabled and neurodivergent artist, designer, writer and alt educator. Her studio practice critically examines the Medical Industrial Complex (MIC) and its subsequent influence over disabled bodies. Emily is a 2024 Ford Foundation, Mellon Foundation and United States Artists Disability Futures Fellow and a 2025 Eames Institute Curious 100. Her work has been featured by institutions such as Carnegie Museum of Art, Institute of Contemporary Art Los Angeles, MoMA, Yale School of Art and more. Emily is the founder of *cripple*, a publishing initiative that supports disabled (including neurodivergent) artists and designers, as well as the creator of the concept Stim Aesthetics and the designer of the 504 Font. Stim Aesthetics is a theoretical framework that examines the influence of both disability and neurodivergence in contemporary art and culture.

Finnegan Shannon is an artist experimenting with forms of access. Some of their recent work includes *Alt Text as Poetry*, a collaboration with Bojana Coklyat that explores the expressive potential of image description; *Do You Want Us Here or Not*, a series of benches and cushions designed for exhibition

spaces; and *Don't mind if I do*, a conveyor-belt-centred exhibition that prioritizes rest and play. Their work has been supported by a Wynn Newhouse Award, an Eyebeam fellowship, a Disability Futures fellowship and grants from Art Matters Foundation, Canada Council for the Arts and the Disability Visibility Project.

Mary Slattery (@invalid__art) is a community organizer, advocate, artist and teacher from Bristol. Her practice is rooted in disability justice and anarchist politics, and she celebrates and centres disabled people's voices and disruptive narratives about their lived experience. Mary collaborates with disabled people around the world to help push conversations and ideas forward.

Grant Stoner is an award-winning reporter covering accessibility and the disabled perspective in the gaming industry. His stories explore accessible innovations from development studios such as Microsoft and PlayStation, as well as reports from the disability community. His work seeks to elevate disabled voices and provide them with a platform that allows them to share their celebrations and concerns.

Jordan Whitewood-Neal is an architectural researcher, designer and educator working at the intersections of architectural history, design pedagogy, disability and spatial justice. Jordan works as a researcher at the Quality of Life Foundation and currently co-leads a design think tank at the London School of Architecture. In 2022 he co-founded disability-led research collective Dis with James Zatka-Haas, exploring disability, storytelling and the built environment.

Clifton Wright's drawings and ceramics stretch and bend the figurative, entangling the laws of anatomy, gravity, time and space. His first major solo exhibition *Hieroglyphics of the Face* at Block 336 in 2022 followed the success of his display at Collect 2022 Somerset House where his drawings and ceramics were acquired by the V&A. Notable group exhibitions include *Time Spaghetti* at Dulwich Picture Gallery (2024), *Lunar Lullabies* at Firstsite, Colchester (2023/4) and *Close: Drawn Portraits* at Drawing Room, London (2018). He joined the Intoart studio in 2005.

Acknowledgements

This book is nothing without its contributors, who spent their time and energy creating this book with us. I'm deeply grateful to have had the chance to make something like this together, which is full of trust, care and joy.

Thank you to our incredible publishing team: Emily Angus (for patience, perseverance and cats), Becca Fortey (for getting us there), and Coralie Hepburn and Tom Windross (for believing in the project, and your understanding). It came together very nicely indeed. Thanks to Joe Ewart for his bold design, and Jessica McCarthy for getting this entire book into shape. Andrew Tullis, thank you for your diligent sleuthing. We are very grateful for all the effort you put in to making sure that every word was taken care of, and that you came on this journey with us.

Design and Disability had its beginnings as an exhibition, but hopefully this book will continue a conversation that started long before us. Thank you to Nigel Bamforth for putting forward the idea at the V&A all those years ago, and Circe Henestrosa for such enthusiasm and creativity in helping it arrive at the door.

Thank you to everyone who helped inform the exhibition that led to the conversations in this book, who talked to me on research trips and video calls, helped with objects, archives and collections, wandered garden and city paths, and shaped our thinking: Rachel Brown, Sinéad Burke, Christine Checinska, Ashley Dalle, Gemma Daw, Rachel Dedman, Chancey Fleet, Esther Fox, Barry Ginley, David Gissen, Beck Heslop, Liz Jackson, Janice Li, Jenny Mabbott, Laurie Britton Newell, Katherine Ott, Meredith Peruzzi, Betsy Pittman, Michael Powell, Cicely Proctor, Drew Robarge, Jonathan Trinque, Bess Williamson and Natalie E. Wright.

I am grateful to our Advisory Group whose guidance and expertise during the making of the exhibition has been vital and whose influence on both me and the institution has been tentacular and infinite. Thank you Zainab Jumoke Abdullahi, Sonia Boué, Elizabeth Guffey, Arjun Harrison-Mann, Louise Hickman, Poppy Levison, Maggie Matić, Kym Oliver, Natasha Trotman, Jordan Whitewood-Neal and Hannah Wallis.

I am indebted to the wise words and actions of Jos Boys and DisOrdinary Architecture, including Mandy Redvers-Rowe, David Redvers-Rowe, Helen Stratford, Chris Laing, Abi Palmer and Zoe Partington, who shaped the design of the exhibition and in turn the V&A of the future.

Thanks to the Disabled Action Group and Neurodiversity Network at the V&A, who have been comrades and critical friends through the making of this exhibition and book. I would be nowhere without the constant and unwavering support of the Design and Digital team, Corinna Gardner, Melanie Lenz, Donata Miller-Obebe and William Seung, who have been champions of this project and kept us going with love and snacks. Also to Chris Turner for his support and to Nazek Ghaddar for keeping AAPD going.

This book would not exist without the exhibition, for which I thank Cat Macdonald, Anaïs Goorriah, Olivia Oldroyd and Phoebe Evans, who made the entire thing possible. Sam Brown, Anne Zhou, Kirsten Abildgaard and Jed Fielder, thank you for getting it and taking care every step of the way. Asha McLoughlin, Rachel Flaxman and Muriel Bryans, I am grateful for your openness and for coming with us.

Reuben Liebeskind, you gave such an immense amount of care, pride and thought to every stage of this project, I cannot imagine it without your compassion and commitment.

A final thanks and dedication to Station, Philae and Reuben's cat Miso, our emotional support animals, and to Aidan Harris, always.

Natalie Kane, exhibition curator

Image credits